'Not a Fictional Mum lea
and a deep desire to make
behind in the conversatic
hood. The difficult topics
conversations are started as a result. I've learnt so
much from her already and can't wait to see what she
does next.'

Giovanna Fletcher, host of
Happy Mum, Happy Baby podcast

'A fantastic read – funny, clever, heartbreaking and
heart-warming but above all else real and beautifully
written.'

Lisa Faulkner, author of *Meant to Be*

'Incredibly valuable and insightful. Her mission to
invite more, much-needed inclusivity to the narrative
around parenting and the varied journeys towards it,
is delivered with such warmth, passion and compassion that we can't help but want to pick up a flag and
fly it beside her.'

Anna Mathur, author of *Know Your Worth*

'Not a Fictional Mum opened my eyes to a whole
other part of being a mother that is missing from
today's media.'

Rochelle Humes, television presenter

Not a Fictional Mum is a wife, mother and care-experienced campaigner advocating for a community she feels the government is failing. She has campaigned alongside leading UK charities in Westminster regarding the current self-employed adopter's legislation and headed a petition exceeding 16,000 signatures, securing a parliamentary debate. She professes to be an 'accidental' writer who, despite having written over 62,000 words about her life, still finds writing an 'author bio' somewhat bizarre. She tips her pen to every child of the care system, past, present and future, and offers words of hope and courage to those trying to reach parenthood. She is represented by the Hardman & Swainson literary agency and *What Makes a Mum?* is her first book.

What
Makes
a Mum?

My Story
From Fostered
to Adopter

Not a Fictional Mum

unbound

First published in 2024

Unbound
c/o TC Group, 6th Floor King's House, 9–10 Haymarket,
London SW1Y 4BP
www.unbound.com
All rights reserved

Text design by Jouve (UK), Milton Keynes

A CIP record for this book is available from the British Library

ISBN 978-1-80018-304-9 (paperback)
ISBN 978-1-80018-305-6 (ebook)

Printed and bound in Great Britain by Bell & Bain Ltd, Glasgow

3 5 7 9 8 6 4 2

With thanks to the patrons of this book:

CCS Adoption

The Fertility Show

The Modern Family Show

Emma Astley, Lillie-Beth Astley,
Chris Astley, Cameron Astley, Oliver Astley

For any stranger that has ever cared.
All the miniature Spiderthem
And every Orca in my pod,
I love you.

At the start of writing this book there
were over 80,000 children in
the UK care system.

All names in this book have been anonymised,
including my own, to protect identities.

Any content surrounding infertility diagnoses
or insights as to why children are placed for
adoption are universal and have been
taken from professional sources
indexed throughout the book.

Miscarriage will be mentioned and there
will be an italicised warning under
the chapter heading.

I have published this memoir in hope of my
personal story being supportive to others.
It is a recollection of events from *my* life,
as I remember them.

Please respect my choice of anonymity to
respectfully protect others.

Contents

Contents

Prologue

I'm NFM. Not a Fictional Mum, perfectionist and self-professed serial planner. I like to plan most aspects of my life. I would *love* to plan most aspects of everyone else's life if they let me, but they don't. I'm an introverted extrovert. A Local Authority Care Leaver but so much more than that acronym. A mother related only by love and a daughter without a mother. I've received strains of maternal love from unexpected sources and learnt to love myself. I like to have friends but not too many. I like surprises, but preferably planned ones, and snack on dark chocolate with a slice of Granny Smith.

I've lived a life less 'ordinary', some might say, but that's the exact narrative I want to challenge. We live in a blended society, we embrace and celebrate that being the case, but are we informed enough?

I've felt alone at times, and I don't like the thought of others feeling that isolation. Let my story walk beside those who need a friend. I've written this at a time when there is a record number of children in care and a national shortage of foster carers. I've written it because there isn't enough honesty concerning infertility treatment and to help alleviate some of the fears and misconceptions about adoption. I've written it because we're here for only a snapshot in time and the only offerings I have to contribute to change are my advocacy, my solidarity and the hard-won understanding from my lived experience.

A tale of two halves: my less conventional experiences of being mothered, and trying to reach motherhood. *My* life. I've chosen to share some of it, as my offering towards a more informed society. At the very least opening up much-needed conversations surrounding alternative routes to parenthood, the UK childcare system and this thing called love. All I ask in return is for you to read it respectfully, taking off your shoes before you step onto the pages.

When I look back and see myself as a little girl, I feel heavy. I feel the weight of sadness through every part of my body. Then I see her floating away, with her head of thick, brown curls and little feet in blue leather shoes. I want to reach out and hold her hand, I want to mother myself and tell her it's going to be tough but she will be strong enough, brave enough, braver than her one-eyed, orange teddy she so aptly named 'Jaffa'. He was her confidant, she thought him very valiant. Although she failed to recognise that behind every brave teddy stands an even stronger child.

I used to scuttle away from the chaos, like a cockroach. Damn, I have the sexiest descriptive for myself. I am a bit of a cockroach, though. I reckon if a nuclear bomb went off, I'd still find a way to come scuttling out of the ruins. They can be flattened and still go about their roachy business, you know, holding onto both pairs of their wings, folding them neatly over their back. Researchers discovered they can still run nearly as fast while squished. Their maternal approach has served their offspring well for the past 125 million years; they can live for one whole week without their head and hold their breath for up to forty minutes. Both of which I think I definitely had a go at during my childhood and quest to reach motherhood.

The one thing this cockroach always assumed was that, when she felt ready, motherhood would just arrive for her, simply turn up banging on the window like that neighbour you're not all that keen on but they still insist on flashing their gnashers at you every time they walk past. (*Gnashers*, not knickers, although I'd probably warm to them a tad more if they did start doing that.)

I'm sure it won't shock you all that much now to hear how I had a life plan. That's what some adult children of dysfunction just *love* to do. *Plan stuff*, a bid to try to take back a bit of control. Meals, social calendar, your neighbours' loft conversion, which day of the week you're permitting yourself a sweet treat. I couldn't get enough of it, like a cat sniffing round your legs for one of those foul-smelling astronaut food pouches. Don't get me wrong, I still look forward to my wild pic 'n' mix Saturdays, the suspense of not knowing exactly which jelly will be pulled from that pot. It's still the same old me. I'm just more consciously aware and let my neighbours choose their own en-suite.

The simple truth is that you *cannot* plan every aspect of your life. Sorry if I'm crushing dreams here, but you just can't. Granted, you can make some good decisions: green tea, sleep – all the exciting stuff. Aside from what you choose to consume and the time you take yourself to bed, the rest of it is simply beyond our control. We're all on a voyage of sorts, that's what I've come to believe. We've evolved slightly more than the average primate and been left on this massive piece of spherical crust to get on with it. To make sense of the nonsensical, survive and, in among making it through another day, fill our souls with whatever it is that makes us happy. We're mammals and mammals like to love and be loved, don't they? I'm not really that hairy but I wanted that, I wanted to know love and to love. The exact strain of love I wanted to understand and to reach was that of the maternal kind. Motherhood, #mumlife, call it what you will, I needed to get acquainted with it.

Anyway, just for the craic, here was 'the life plan':

- Try to have a functional childhood.
- Replace Geri in the Spice Girls, or, failing that, Mutya in the Sugababes.
- Obtain a career I actually enjoyed and wouldn't leave me surviving on Turkey Twizzlers for the rest of my days. (Note to self and reader: writing a book probably won't resolve this.)
- Meet a sporty hunk, get married.
- Live at the same address for over five years, so I can complete application forms in a more timely manner.
- Start a family before the age of thirty.

Only two and a half of those came through – I still have to enjoy the odd Twizzler come the end of the month. It's at this point I feel I ought to let you know I'm not writing under an alias as Mutya or Geri. In fact, I don't share my name, I've chosen not to. Among more personal reasons, I have a longstanding gripe with our discriminatory political system and enjoy reminding them that I'm NOT A FICTIONAL MUM (I'll share the why behind that later), but the gist of it is, I won't be sharing my name, and if a guy can go round spray painting some of the most influential pieces of modern art without sharing his and I'm not actually defacing anything, I think we can all roll along here just fine. Call me NFM for short.

P.S. Banksy, I absolutely love you.

P.P.S. Like, so much, and I wish you would come round and deface the side of my house or even my whole house.

I own my house.

So I can invite him over to do that.

One thing I do not own, the thing none of us actually *own*, is our children.

I fear we do that as a society, you know, see children as things we own, something we gain an immediate right to claim possession of; an extension of ourselves almost. But I believe no human being is an extension of another – how can we be? We arrive and we depart as ourselves.

Giving birth to a biological child is the social norm, the procreation process we are often conditioned to feel more comfortable with. Let's face it, any routes to parenthood other than this are less familiar, intriguing, complicated, complex, not clear-cut enough, straight down the line enough, 'conventional' enough. Surely all routes to parenthood should be part of the conventional message from day dot?

Ask yourself. How familiar were you with 'alternative' or 'non-traditional' family units when you were growing up? The common reality of family breakdowns, strangers caring for children, children caring for adults, parental estrangement, same sex parenting, the concept of not being able to have children, childlessness, assisted fertility, or the power of unrelated love. We would have all had some exposure to this, if not through personal experience, then within families or friendship groups. It certainly wasn't coming from education or the media. Alternative and non-traditional family structures have always existed in some capacity.

Hopefully one day we won't need to make reference to 'alternative' or 'non-traditional' either.

Just families.

In a sense we're told what motherhood is, aren't we? Influenced, not in the literal sense but subliminally, through the power of media, social media, Hollywood, *Hello!* magazine, whatever you're into. We're conditioned to believe how it looks and what it is, and the truth of the matter is, it's not been all that inclusive. We're living in the modern era, so let's leave the linear approach to what family really means back there with the dinosaurs, shall we?

For a child like me who had received only fragments

of mothering, this Hollywood ideology only left me feeling excluded and a bit odd.

There was a wall I would sit on as a child after school, by way of prolonging a deliciously sugary Wham bar and the trip home. I didn't always want to go home. It was just your standard sort of wall, bricks, the odd weed sprouting through here and there, cold and uncomfortable on the nether regions, nothing really to report on the wall front. It was what was on the other side that often held my attention. There was a huge square meterage of perfectly kept grass, the type you would hoover if you had it. On certain days the odd toy would be scattered around, wooden ones (back then, wooden toys were associated with the wealthy, you couldn't get them in the Aldi middle aisles). On the other side of the carpet grass stood a house. A beautiful white house with a huge window, perfect for a child stalker like me.

Behind the window lived a family. A mum, dad and two small children. It's at this stage I'm desperately hoping that a) they never saw me and b) my face has matured significantly since childhood. The mum had bouncy hair; Dad was often in a suit. Sometimes they would come out into the garden, at which point I would shit myself and try to morph into a brick. The mother was usually happy throughout most of these viewings. Not ecstatic, bouncing off the walls happy, just, you know, averagely happy. It wasn't her being happy that intrigued me, it was more her mood being consistent.

It all seemed so simple.

How it *should* be.

I never saw her screaming, in between manically laughing. Or informing her young children on how they would come to reach their deaths through the medium of a knock-off pack of Tarot cards.

All in all, they seemed pretty 'normal'. (My life savings – which I haven't started yet – to the first person who can tell me what that even means.)

So, I would sit on walls accompanied by half-eaten Wham bars watching the stark contrast to my home life feeling like I was the only person living in anything less than the stereotypical 2.4 with a white picket fence.

What fed my desire to believe that's just how it was for everyone else?

American TV, that's what.

American TV families with their perfect lawns, white houses, large windows and moms with bouncy hair. Cheering on their offspring during Californian sports days while handing out cups of Sunny D. I bought into that bull crap, and it still angers me now. I mean, look, I'm sure they were a perfectly lovely functioning family; I have no evidence to prove otherwise, and lord knows I sat staring at them enough. But my point is: I could very well just have been seeing what I'd been conditioned to see.

A kid coping with the chaos.

While admittedly I was envious of their house and carpet grass, I was yearning for their *happiness*. Connection and consistency.

Let this be a story of resilience, hope and beautiful complexities. Let it educate, provoke thought, question convention, and, above all else, explore the question:

What makes a mum?

Beefy

I've never really liked beef. I can't stand the smell of it cooking. I won't comment on the taste of a steak as it has never made it that far. However, I have a joint of beef memory, one which I'm pretty certain is unique, and it reminds me that my childhood was anything but conventional.

My mother had a real issue with this particular joint (some would say she had some beef). This wasn't just any joint, you see; *this* was a joint apparently poisoned by my father. A soon-to-be defrosted succulent piece of meat sprinkled with arsenic and lashings of peppercorn sauce.

It wasn't.

We couldn't afford peppercorn sauce.

It might still have been frozen but was most definitely poison-free. I recall many conversations like this growing up; my mother suffered from different symptoms at various points throughout my childhood. It was a stigmatised generation surrounding mental health. I was personally mistaken for the devil on more than one occasion and was debriefed on the acceptable amount of time she could be in Tesco before I should call forensics to check if she'd been buried under the frozen peas. Admittedly, I now know it can get pretty tense down those special buy aisles.

Of course, this isn't funny, none of it is. It's really bloody tragic. Nor did I have the capacity to understand or empathise with what she was going through at that time. Mental illness or other disturbance has the power to bulldoze lives, demolish relationships and tear apart families, dragging both individuals and anyone on the side-lines along for the ride.

It happens though. Hallucinations, delusions and dysfunction, topped off with my father's alcohol addiction and a decent enough stint for me in foster care. It was what it was.

I don't know how else to write it.

I won't ever forget this beefy suspect. I can't because Beefy arrived the evening before she walked out. The day my mother left. My sister and I proudly returned from the corner shop clutching a multipack of Space Raiders; if you made it back from the Spar any time after 2 p.m. on some of the estates where we lived with your Raiders still intact, it really was a quest to be proud of. Only to discover she'd gone.

Vanished.

Evaporated.

The evening before, she had barricaded herself into the spare room. From what I could make out she was convinced that this innocent piece of beef, simply chilling in the freezer (as joints do), was going to be responsible for her ending. In my immaturity and immunity to these outbursts, I took the joint from the freezer and named him 'Beefy', before acting out an interrogation scene between the joint and an oven glove.

'*Do you have any drugs on you?*'

'*It's just garlic cloves, I promise.*'

I've always pratted around during times of inconsolable pain. It was and still is an inconsolable pain because it's abandonment, isn't it? At least that's how I experienced it as a child. So, I've always tried to make everyone laugh, played the class clown. People *like* funny people, they have *time* for funny people.

I know what you're thinking: what has this got to do with my journey through infertility or adoption? All right, we get she doesn't like beef (hardly the biggest shocker during generation vegan), but we want to know if there's any hope. We want to hear about the tens of thousands of people who want to become parents and have to live with the potential terror of never reaching motherhood. We get you had a difficult childhood but what has that really got to do with *this*? Fear not, my trusty passengers, that is coming, but let us not be naïve. This part matters; it matters greatly. It matters because once I'd laid my genetics to rest, I needed to go back and make peace with my biological past.

I want to take you through the evolution of both my understanding and reaching motherhood.

Hold on, take courage.

Oprah

My husband is incredible. Let's start right there. One of those people you're honoured to cross paths with in life, he's a thinker, a talker, a never judge anyone before you've listened type, just a damn beautiful soul and in my opinion, the best-looking giant dancing chameleon I've ever seen. (You're going to need to read on to make any sense of that.) He's also not once tried to talk me out of an idea. No matter how wacky, far-fetched or bizarre, unless he thinks it's really shite, and then he has no qualms in telling me that's the case. More often than not, he's my wingman, from the time he dressed up as Lord Grantham for my *Downton Abbey*-themed thirtieth, to the day I turned to him and said I wouldn't be returning to my soul-destroying, target-driven, corporate career spanning seven years because I wanted to campaign for equality and recognition for *all* families. He's always right there beside me, walking around the BBC costume hire department or correcting the spelling in my book proposal. He has *always* been there.

We met on the day Whitney Houston died. She was wonderful, wasn't she? Just pure magnificence. I wanted to go out and celebrate her life. Don my shoulder-padded jacket, pink lipstick, and dance. So, I did just that.

The same day England beat France in Paris in the Six Nations.

'Twas also a Sunday.

We all know what kind of late-night watering holes are open on the Sabbath. I feel no need to expand. We met in one of those.

He comes over, asks if I want a drink. I'm skint and absolutely parched, so politely accept. He proceeds to ask if I would prefer a long or a short beverage. I have no idea what he's on about, but long sounds like more value for his money and I'm considerate like that. He's tall, dark and handsome. Genuinely. Six foot four, dark brown hair and eyes, with a jawline that makes *Beauty and the Beast*'s Gaston look like Rubble from *Paw Patrol*. I can see he's older than me; he's also totally leathered and has a male sidekick in tow who is effortlessly sliding down the wall of the DJ booth.

He's quite serious, bit intense, actually. Total opposite from *joke yourself happy* over here. He asks how I would feel about dating an older man (cocky, like it). I remind him that I'm not and have absolutely zero intentions of doing so. He says he wouldn't mind kissing me. I tell him to piss off.

It's perfect.

I've noted he mentioned how he had been

watching the rugby so decide to ask him if he a) knows how to do the Hakka and b) if he would be so kind as to show me.

He can't slam that short drink down quick enough. He stands in front of me with utter conviction, eyes fixed upon mine; he tries to shrink himself a bit as he squats himself into position and peels one large canoe foot at a time from the sticky dance-floor, chanting:

Hump-e-ty Dump-e-ty
Sat on a wall
Hump-e-ty Dump-e-ty
Had a great fall.
All the king's hors . . .

His stare intensifies even further, he flails his hands wildly around and for the grand finale sticks his tongue out like a giant, dancing chameleon.

I thought, 'My God! He's attractive,' gave him my phone number and ran off.

Now, my nicknames, I've had a few, 'Ice-Queen', 'Love-able Cactus', and 'Commander Spiffing' still being my all-time fave mainly because it's enabled me to play up to this narrative over the years. I'm quite well spoken, you see; I'll explain how that came to be later, but the prospect of *anyone* thinking I'd come from total privilege has admittedly given me quite the cheap thrill. We live in a society where family breakdowns, addiction, dysfunction and stints in foster care don't happen to those who overenunciate, apparently. In close second, we have 'The Ice-Queen'. By far the most popular of the two and, I have to admit, a really rather accurate moniker.

I couldn't trust, *wouldn't* love, and really wasn't the biggest fan of, people.

I'm not about to get all deep and arty (fans herself down with a quill), just saying it how it was. I needed to get that off my chest because this next part still, even to this day, makes no logical sense.

Our first date went well. We met outside Waga-mama, both of us desperately trying to remember what the other actually looked like. A considerable amount of both long and short drinks had been consumed that first night, so there was every chance we could have ended up sharing a noodle with any one of the randoms lined up outside Waggas. Each of us in the same position, nervously waiting to meet the stranger they'd liaised with just a few nights before. Hoping their beer goggles didn't disappoint over a duck pancake and that neither one of us was secretly a serial killer. He was telling me how some woman had been stalking him at the gym; I asked him if he'd ever read *Get Happy*, Judy Garland's biography. I came to the conclusion that he was really rather odd; he thought I was some arty, overprivileged brat who was descended from a bloodline of aristocrats. We were quite taken by one another. After finishing our chicken infused noodles, we dragged out the short walk back to my humble dwellings, shared a little smooch on the doorstep before I said goodbye and shut the front door. I'm classy like that, would never expect anyone to shut the door for me.

He was hooked; must have been all the talk of Judy and Mr Sinatra's sexual encounter in the toilets. He messaged me that evening asking if I would like to meet up later that week, suggesting the cinema. There was no doubt I wanted to see him again. We rather picturesquely had the entire cinema to ourselves. I'd picked a bit of easy viewing, opting for a British comedy drama. He was OK with this decision after I'd explained the longstanding crush I had on Bill Nighy, the supremely talented actor who was far older than him, leaving him bounding out of the cinema with a notably younger spring in his step.

I think they call it an epiphany, don't they? A moment of sudden and great revelation. That's exactly what I had while sitting in that desolate cinema, just a few weeks after the tragic passing of one of the best-selling music artists of all time. I looked to this man (not Bill, the younger one chewing on a jelly snake) and thought *I'm going to marry this person*. I mean, come on, *how odd* is that? We weren't even talking to each other in there for a start. I remember really enjoying just sitting next to him, he made me feel really *safe*, and up until this moment, I'd never noticed I wanted or even needed to feel that. I'd struggled to sit through a whole film or read an entire book most of my life, only not when I sat next to him. I felt oddly *relaxed*, a relatively new sensation, and not because he was tall (I could have hung out with a giraffe for comfort if it was purely down to stature). There was just something about him, the way he was, his energy, aura, spirit, whatever it was. I liked it, a lot.

I didn't tell him about this epiphany, obviously. Instead, I decided to ignore his advances over the next few days, for fear I might have been thawing. I made out I had just a tad more on than I did; mind you, it's really rather time-consuming watching entire seasons of *Catfish* within a weekend timeframe with only a box of Cheerios for company. I also need to let you know that this *I'm going to marry you* mindset wasn't a regular occurrence for me with men. It certainly didn't happen with the earlier date I'd had that same afternoon in Caffè Nero.

All I can put it down to is luck. I was really very lucky to have simply been dancing in the right place at the right time. One of life's jackpot moments not everybody will have, *that* and of course Whitney Elizabeth Houston, and so, for the amalgamation of all the above, I remain eternally very grateful.

Fast forward a decent number of years, wonderful *husband* and I are in a therapy session. I'm sitting on one edge of a purposefully selected, smaller-than-average sofa, holding a beige cushion with silver leafing detail; to the left is a strategically placed box of tissues. They're strategic because the top one has been semi-pulled from the opening, for speedy, emotional breakdown access. My husband is sitting a good five centimetres away from me, which, just to reiterate, is the furthest he *can* physically sit from me. He's created a chin perch with his hand by resting an elbow on the side of the sofa, his legs horizontally stretched, one ankle resting upon the other. He had nice shoes on during this particular session. I remember really wanting to be annoyed with him: our last IVF cycle hadn't worked and because I love him, it's *him* I decided to take it all out on. So I was very disappointed with myself for having such moments of weakness, internally complimenting his shoes.

Here we were, your very own answer to Burton and Taylor (my book, my analogy), the couple who fell madly in love, engaged after a year, married after two, had a wedding so sickeningly stylish it earned itself a feature in a wedding magazine (permission to spew), telling our infertility counsellor how we couldn't have sex with each other any more because I would start crying halfway through at the prospect of never becoming a mum and, as it turns out, my husband isn't remotely interested in having sex with crying women.

It's safe to say, Oprah was about to earn her money. (Disclaimer: Oprah Winfrey was not our infertility counsellor. In a bid to support anonymity for all involved there will be nicknames throughout, this being one of them.)

Of course, the most recent failed cycle wasn't his fault, none of them were. A failed cycle is no one's 'fault'. It comes back to that lottery of life, a successful roll of the dice, a good run on the slot machines, and science. You need a good old-fashioned batch of healthy eggs, a strong dollop of sperm and lashings of science. Put the lucky charms, socks and dream catchers away, ain't none of that gonna get you a BFP (big fat positive – stole that one from the forums I'd become privy to in the past few years). You need cash and plenty of it, the psychological resilience of an SAS operative and whatever goods it is you can bring to the operating table.

It was during this session that I made reference to my own mother, a relationship that, up until this point, I'd rarely allowed myself to think about. There's nothing like the prospect of your genetics coming to the end of the line to get you in the mood for a full-on family reunion. I shared how I'd been thinking about her, I wasn't really sure *why*, but for the first time in my adult life, I had, and it was this thinking that was now leading me to questions and questions now wanting answers. They do say thinking's dangerous, don't they?

I liked this therapist (I've had a few), firstly because she refrained from looking at the clock during our sessions, or if she did, she'd totally bloody mastered the art of doing it incognito. For that skill alone I was happy to keep paying. Credit where credit's due. And secondly, she stayed clear of that ever-so-slightly patronising therapist nod with the occasional *hmm* chucked in for good therapist measure.

I liked her because, rightly or wrongly, she would sometimes offer an insight. Be it personal or professional I won't ever actually know, but she offered some and by this stage of our infertility journey that's *exactly* what I needed. She enlightened me on how it's really not that uncommon for patients facing the closing of their infertility journey, estranged from their families, to feel a desire to make peace with their genetic past.

Told you.

G E N I U S.

Who The Hell Am I?

Since Oprah's latest session, I kept thinking about my mother, her face, her teeth – she had nice teeth. I would have flashbacks of us all dancing up and down the stairs singing 'Alice the Camel', she frantically waving a wooden abacus around. I hoped it would pass; I wasn't actively seeking any more cans of worms to open up here. I don't enjoy navigating my way through more than a ton of shit at any one time. Only it doesn't, it doesn't *go away*. If all I'm ever going to genetically see of myself is to be within my own reflection, if I may never have the opportunity of motherhood, of giving a child the stability and love with no contract that I had been hoping to give for so long, then I really did need to go back and get some answers from the woman who was responsible for my early onset greys and who didn't even grant me a goodbye before she walked out of my life.

Growing into my late teens and early adult years I very rarely missed her. That's possibly the most tragic part to my childhood story, the fact that she'd gone but I really wasn't all that devastated.

I was relieved.

I felt like I could breathe when she left. I can remember hearing my own breath, the inhale, the sound of my lungs expanding and the steadiness of its release. She was suffocating, stifling actually, because she was frightened. If I had to compare her to an object (which I'm aware no one's asking me to do but I've always loved a visual aid), she was like a pillow.

Confusing things, pillows; soft, comforting, the thing you gravitate towards when it all becomes too much. They also have the potential to suffocate you, don't they? With help, I mean, not on their own. What I'm trying to say is that how she suffered was the constant drive behind what I felt was her suffocation of my personality, my whole being, the stifled household in which I grew up. There was no freedom to express, no opinions of your own, the only comfort you felt you could turn to would turn itself on you whenever it took its fancy. When it was soft, though, it was nice; I liked it.

Undeniably, there were personal moments of sporadic anger and jealousy that made an appearance from time to time. I can remember the exact moment I started my period, a couple of weeks after she had left. I was about to step into a scalding hot bath; never seen the point of the water expenditure on a lukewarm one, as I like to come out looking like a lobster. One foot had been dunked into the lava bath, the other still resting on a bright blue bathmat. As I looked down at the aquatic themed material, I noticed I was bleeding. I just stood there, staring at it. My right foot just bubbling away. I didn't know what to do. I had a dad downstairs who, although we had resided together all my life, I didn't really *know* all that well. That was a part of how she could be, stifling loyalty. You had to prove you were loyal to her, that you only loved *her*. There was no allowance to love both parents equally. You were on her team, or you weren't, and if you weren't, you would know about it.

I wrapped a discoloured towel around my body, sat on the toilet and cried. Really cried, and I think that was the first time I had done so since she left. One of my friends at school had a posh, silver zipped cosmetic pouch with scented lavender bags inside stuffed with an array of pastel-coloured period accessories bearing a striking resemblance to a bag of pick 'n' mix. Her mum had sorted it all for her and she'd been carrying it around for months in preparation for the big day. Her mother had the ability to actually give a functional crap about her daughter's pubescent years. In that moment I felt deep envy. I wanted a mother, not *mine* necessarily, just one who would be able to help me navigate my way through these next few years. The final years of secondary school, my GCSEs, the Prom, which in most teens' world is just about the only life event that even matters.

I'd questionably ruined the towel. I opened the bathroom door and shouted down to my dad. As he looked up at me from the bottom of the uncarpeted stairs of the newest residence she had just moved us all into, I told him I'd started my period. He replied with a flustered '*Right, OK*' and scurried off to the nearest Londis.

In my lived experience you can accept something is over when you have some understanding of *why*, proof even. We can accept someone is dead once we see the body or coffin; part of the reason we have a funeral is to grieve, right? To have something to symbolise the end. Only *she* hadn't died; my hope of a functional mother had. I guess it expired before I was even born. There were puzzle pieces missing that I really needed but simply didn't have; I would spend the next decade of my life scuttling along, holding my breath, sometimes with my head, sometimes without, just an angry, distrusting, motherless cockroach. I guess that's what coming to the end of our infertility journey prompted, the domino effect to the accumulation of my grief, the instinctive need for *closure*.

Before I move on. Thank you to the woman who did help me choose my prom dress. The stranger who invited me into her home, taught me how to dispose of a sanitary towel properly and introduced me to gammon and pineapple.

The stranger who supported me with a girl's two most important dress choices in life. Upon hearing I was getting married, tracking me down many years after I moved out. Sending a cheque nestled into a little note reading 'For your dress' accompanied by two small silver, heart-shaped teaspoons. I hadn't spoken to you for almost a decade, but you didn't forget me. I think you've always quite liked me but this gesture felt more than it being just that. Maybe you knew I would always be the adult child of an angry and frightened young girl who needed to know she mattered.

I am and she did.

Now I need to take this moment to let you know just how truly fantastic you are.

And to thank you in the book I never imagined writing, for playing me down the aisle on my wedding day.

You played me through every step, quite literally, from the church gallery while I nervously held the steady hand of my dad, walking right beside me.

Not your generic wedding party but a God-damn beautiful one.

Back to the accumulative grief.

Shortly after the world's most insightful therapy session, my husband and I had stepped into an Enid Blyton-style adventure. The many-years-after-she's-walked-out version, where I suddenly decide to do a bit of soul searching. I could have taken a gap year, ridden an elephant, felt unethical about it then started a crowd-funding page. Instead, I decided to try to track her down, searching less in caves and pebbled beaches, more in laundrettes, social clubs and boozers. I knew the area; I'd heard through the powers of social media roughly where she lived but had no actual address. Too curious, that's another of my personality traits, not to be confused with nosey. As a child, I wasn't aware of any diagnosis for my mother's behaviour. I thought she was eccentric, charismatic, unpredictable, spiteful, funny, intimidating, beautiful, manipulative and, at times, bloody great fun. Some days I would turn the key in the lock after school and she would be suggesting we paint rainbows on our bedroom floors having just baked a batch of warm, sugary treats. On others, she hadn't quite made it out of her own bedroom. I was a young teen when she left, a woman by the time I went back and felt ready some answers. They didn't even need to be verbal, I just needed to see the situation through adult lenses.

I fell in love with my husband a little bit more that afternoon. Taking my hand, marching beside me (into laundrettes, newsagents, and some of the less friendly bars I've experienced), asking if anyone knew of a woman by her name. What's absolutely bat shit (shouldn't joke about bat shit; I started writing this book during the Covid-19 pandemic – that's what we all did, started writing books) is that in the last place we asked, some guy *actually knew her*. He knew where she lived, and even more *cat* shit? He guessed I was her daughter. I looked like her, apparently. Of course, I do, but I'd emotionally estranged myself from that fact for all these years. *Now* here was a total stranger looking me dead in the eyes seeing a resemblance.

It was weird.

A stark reminder that I couldn't detach myself entirely.

I did get *some* answers that day and what I will say is this:

A parent who's intimidating to their child doesn't look as scary when the girl grows up.

My mother was a child once.

A teenager.

A young woman.

Before she became a mother, she was all of these things.

Maybe a child who liked to play make-believe, run along beaches, stare at clouds in the sky, laugh, eat ice-lollies. Whittling away those childhood hours allowing her imagination to run wild. Only now I wonder how wild it was left to run.

Children's imaginations are quite simply pure, artistic genius. Unedited, uninhibited, unfiltered craziness. *That's* what makes them so bloody fantastic. I recall many an afternoon lost in jungles, locked in towers and starring in sell-out tours (globally). It's escapism, isn't it? Nature's way of protecting children, ensuring they don't spend their precious childhood days bogged down by the trivia of life (unlike the adults around them). A safe space, a private confidential corner of your mind.

Imagine if that was invaded, trespassed, someone just waltzed on in with a giant can of aerosol and graffitied all over your thoughts.

A child held hostage inside their own mind.

And if it didn't start then, does it make it any less terrifying as an adolescent? The few pictures I have, the innocence in the one of her and my father, not much more than kids themselves, sporting overgrown barnets, arms rested on each other's shoulders, twinning in their Guns N' Roses t-shirts, blissfully unaware of the emotional hurricanes about to rip their way through their marriage over the next dog's age, tells me it can't have been.

I'm not about to try to blame religion for all of this, not intellectual enough. I still can't work out my BCS from my ADS. I am, however, relieved we no longer live in a society where shoving two teens up the aisle because they've got pregnant is deemed a better life decision than extended family gracefully taking a pew downgrade, not giving a hoot to being the congregation's hot topic and actually considering the best method of support for all human beings (born and unborn) involved. God might like you even more for that.

At what point did the children who became adults who became parents feel they could ask for help?

At what crisis point did the adults who had the children who became parents ask them if they needed any?

On reflection they were only two adult children of their own childhoods.

Have I ever hated them?

No.

Blamed them?

Sometimes.

I didn't sleep for nights after I saw her again, listening to my heart pounding through my eardrums wondering what the hell had just gone on. I replayed it all, her opening the door asking who the hell I was, before realising who the hell I was, then inviting us both in for a cuppa. I thought about her hands, her teeth, her hair. I saw her living room, her bathroom, and the empty tea and coffee canisters in the kitchen.

I thought about the way she tried to touch me and how unwanted that was.

I thought about how screwed up and devastatingly sad it all was.

I thought about motherhood.

She asked if I would write.

I said I couldn't.

She asked if I'd forgiven her.

I said no.

She asked if I loved her.

I said yes.

'The Others'

'What are we doing then? Are we trying not to, or just sort of, accidentally on purpose going for it?'

A conversation I remember us having only a few weeks after we got married. We'd initially spoken about waiting in a sensible bid to try to exterminate some of that greenfly on the money tree at the bottom of the garden after the big day. But after a contraceptive-free week away on honeymoon, all that coconut water and sand had influenced us into sacking off the gas bill and prioritising what pram we were going to buy instead.

Not once did it ever cross my mind that I wouldn't get pregnant. Honestly, not once, which does still surprise me when I think about it. I now know that one in seven couples may have difficulty conceiving, so that's at least ten couples at a wedding reception of 140 people, isn't it? Yet, I never knew that before. I'd never even heard of these stats. I was aware cancer will impact at least one in two of us in our lifetime, I knew that heart disease is the leading cause of death, but I honestly did not know that struggling to get pregnant was a far more common societal issue than it's given air-time for. The powerhouse that is Jessica Hepburn named infertility as 'the silent pandemic of the modern world' and she's right and it's because it is so silent that a woman like me just assumed pregnancy would happen. Read her books, by the way, they're important.

NHS Wales claims 'about 84 per cent of couples will conceive naturally within a year if they have regular unprotected sex (every two or three days)'.[1]

What's happened to the other 16 per cent?

We had the love story, the media-worthy wedding. Got the semi decorated to a high standard, feature walls, open-plan kitchen, bit of decking, pot plants, you know the drill. Secured careers, built up a good circle of friends and had exemplary credit scores. We were so ready, we needn't even bother having sex; I should have just noted I was pregnant one morning over my Nespresso machine, an immaculate conception for being so organised.

Only we *were* bothering, a lot. There was scheduling, charts, trackers and ovulation kits. Lying upside down, rehydrating with pineapple juice, consuming green foods only. That's usually the first kind of crazy shit you start doing when there's a glimmer of an infertility issue on the horizon. Eating green stuff, anything you can get your hands on, grass isn't even safe. Why? Because you recognise very quickly this whole procreation malarky is very much out of your control, but you *can* control your leafy greens intake, so you buy a Nutribullet, hold your nose and pretend to enjoy it. There were all sorts of strange things going on in our house but, month after month, the cramps I would try to deny were happening, the blood I tried to pretend wasn't there, simply was. Every month, for a year.

Something else that starts to develop during this time of scheduled conception attempts is a heightened awareness of what's going on around you. You suddenly become that reliable radio station that never dips out of signal. You can sense which one of your friends is pregnant before she even tells you. You note exactly how many months it took a friend to get pregnant from the date she first mentioned they were trying. You sit on wooden steps together in the sunshine hiding your mouth in the cup of warm tea for fear she might be able to see just how painful it is for you to swallow.

You tolerate the well wishes and stories of a woman who conceived octuplets after two years of trying because she had some acupuncture. You smile and you nod, you take the hugs then you go home, stuff that pillow back inside your mouth and cry your soul out. Because you know. Deep down, something isn't right, that you're not going to make it into the 84 per cent club. I just instinctually knew by this point we would be a part of 'the others'. The ones no one really talks about and most secretly hope they won't become. Let it be known, with hindsight, I'd still only ever want to be me.

We make an appointment with the doctor. It's weirdly exciting; you've somehow managed to convince yourself in simply *attending* an appointment with your GP you're now well on your way to parenthood, and even though you don't wish to be going in to talk about the lack of anything happening, you do feel sort of proactive about the situation. Grown-up almost, because it's a 'family planning' appointment and not the usual tonsillitis. You're going to pop in, tell him you're having regular sex, you know exactly how to do it, there just seems to be some sort of minor issue. He's going to prescribe some baby-making medicine and we'll be off on our merry way, allowing just enough time for a quick detour to Mothercare on the way back.

You dress for the occasion, something that says 'motherly potential'. Even the tone of texts to your spouse takes a more mature stance:

Hi darling (refrain from the usual babe)

Don't forget we have our family planning appointment with the Dr today at 15.10.

15.10, I shall be there. Would you like me to pick up some kale after work?

There's not a lot to write about the appointment itself, no lingering details to draw upon. I have been told every good book needs a bit of lingering but I'm afraid I just don't have it. He had our medical records up on the screen; he knew how long we had been trying (guess the receptionist must have passed that detail on when I made the call). He simply gave us both a look accompanied with a sigh he'd most definitely prescribed to couples who'd sat in his beige chairs before us and said:

'I think it's best we send you both for some tests.'

We leave, slagging the doctor off.

We leave, slagging each other off.

'Well, it's not going to be me. I'm younger than you, my BMI is spot on, and I won the junior poetry competition so I can guarantee it won't be me.'

'Excuse me, but the old man only had to look at my mum to get her pregnant. It can't be me.'

We ignore each other for a few moments, which is really quite difficult in this instance because what you're actually doing is ignoring the only other living, breathing person on the planet right now who is feeling identical levels of anxiety at precisely the same time as you. (I think they call it self-sabotage.) Not long after the initial stand-off we both give in because we've now had this epiphany ourselves. I stare at him and him me, we sit there in silence simply looking at each other. It's a different type of look, the one you give your partner when it simultaneously crosses *both* your minds for the very first time that you might not be able to have children. It's vulnerability and what makes it vulnerable is the flip side to this telepathy we've both just acquired; it means we're both looking to the person who has always been able to offer some comfort in times of panic, only not today. We can't do it for each other today because we're *both* frightened.

She was right, our infertility counsellor. The woman we would become very well acquainted with over the next few years. She was accurate on more than one occasion. She once said: '*Men are like a waffle.*' (Hearing her say that while looking directly at him was worth the £60 alone.) '*The little squares in a waffle and they need to stay in that square, compart-mentalise, check out every part of it, before they can move on.*' The ego-fuelled looks I was giving to Mr Waffle were abruptly wiped off my smug face when she started to compare me to cooked spaghetti, '*interconnected, thinking about all outcomes simultaneously*'. Suddenly the £60 didn't seem quite such good value for money.

And while I'm not one for gender stereotyping people into food groups, in our instance I have to say she was spot on. Spaghetti was my exact mental state at that time, and he made an absolutely spectacular waffle. I want to talk immediately after this appointment about every single possible option and gloriously catastrophise them all. What if we don't even qualify for treatment? If it doesn't work? Or we break up? I have a breakdown; he has a breakdown? He doesn't, he's in search of only the facts. Cold, hard, medical evidence and he's not going to even allow himself to think beyond the next appointment. This stand-off becomes a bit of a running theme and where *it* starts to creep in. The destructive, three's a crowd uninvited guest in your marriage: 'Infertility'.

So, we wait, *he* waits (I speculate), alongside the next couple of weeks of blood tests, scans and him doing his thing in a pot for analysis. We try to respect one another's respective food group and hold onto each other's sanity the best we can.

Now, dear readers, before starting this writing journey, I made the decision to share one couple's journey but wanted to keep a level of anonymity. You see, society has a complete *obsession* with needing to know, exposing almost, which member of the couple has the 'problem'. This has always horrified and fascinated me. Will anything be changed by you knowing? I want you to ask yourselves honestly, will it make any difference to those struggling to conceive if you know the ins and outs of the diagnoses? The very same line we don't cross when delving into people's personal lives has miraculously disappeared when it comes to infertility. Allow me to explain something. Infertility is invasive enough for a couple, it holds no job specification or social requirements, it just jumps out on you, tries to strip you of your self-esteem and run away with your voice. I can promise you, it really is exposing enough without becoming Sunday afternoon's gossip over a leg of lamb.

While I'm offering this educational piece, I suppose I may as well expand my point by saying it really doesn't matter who it is with the problem, if either even do. A) because undiagnosed infertility is a thing and b) if you're in love with someone and they cannot reproduce, then you both have the problem, don't you? A pretty big one. Now for my *pièce de educational résistance*. Infertility treatment has to be the only form of medical intervention in the world whereby it is not only the diagnosed patient who will receive the treatment. Think about it: it may be the male who receives the infertility diagnosis, let's say the sperm is of low motility or count, and surgical sperm recovery is needed. But beyond that point, it will be the *female* body that will have to accept every drug, side effect, sedation for each egg retrieval and to deal with the physical effects of any possible chemical pregnancies and miscarriages. This isn't me even for one millisecond trying to downplay the physical impact and medicinal brutality on the male because that is what this is on any gender – brutal. What I am trying to do is cure a bit of curiosity and, in doing so, avoid anyone else spending precious lunchbreaks crying in toilets because they've been forced to contrive answers to questions they should never have been asked.

To clarify, it doesn't make it any easier for the person who didn't get the red card. They both suffer, make sacrifices and cry into their pillows at night. Curiosity didn't *actually* kill the cat, but it *could* kill the little piece of self-esteem someone is clutching onto.

Sprinkle that with your mint sauce next Sunday.

Que Sera, Sera

I'd wanted to get my teeth whitened for years. Not like denture white or rolled a Tipp-Ex mouse across your gnashers white, just enough of the magic stuff to get rid of the coffee stains and actually enjoy catching my fangs' reflection in the rear-view mirror. I'd also accrued a bit of childless disposable income by this point and was in search of some emotional spending in a bid to avoid addressing my actual feelings.

I remember everything about that tooth whitening trip, clear as a gapped tooth whistle. My husband drove me down to the spa hotel offering cosmetic treatments. We were happy that day. By *happy*, I mean we'd taken a temporary break from talking about the fertility test results we were waiting on which nearly always ended in some sort of passively aggressive conversation. The type you don't label as the common 'row', but passive or not, you're airing out your dirty laundry as much as the next couple. We were laughing a lot, not an unusual occurrence. We were early so decided to continue whatever utter ridiculousness we had been finding funny in the car. He's up for the craic,

my husband, always has been, and as I've said before,
I've spent years clowning around, so the two of us
together have whiled away many hours impersonating, embarrassing and laughing at one another. In fact,
the most useful piece of advice we'd been given on our
marriage guidance course (no prizes for guessing
which one of us scheduled in the course) was '*You
want to know the key to a successful union? Make
each other laugh.*' Not particularly the most mind-
bending piece of intellectual wisdom but damn useful
nonetheless. He (Tod, the vicar) went on to say how in
his experience if you could still manage to make each
other laugh or, at the very least, crack a smile at the
end of a hard day then you might just end up one of
those couples sharing a cod lot on the seafront together
from the comfort of your wheelchairs. That's a lifetime aspiration of mine, or at least it was until I
watched Netflix's *Seaspiracy*, which put me off eating
fish for life and now I just live in hope of a nibble on
one of my husband's salty chips. Guilty, your honour,
'twas I who enrolled us. Thought it would offer some
assistance in the long-term marriage plan I'd already
drafted up.

He had a point, though, old Tod; life can be tough,
can't it? Beautiful, magical, reactive, painful and at
times plain rough. Laughter helps; have you noticed
how children struggle to continue their tantrum if
you succeed in making them laugh, if you help them
release that stress hormone with a dollop of dopa-
mine? I hate to bring up Judy's biography *Get Happy*
again, but I was sold my copy purely on the title.

My God, have we laughed; we've laughed when appropriate and during times that were admittedly less so. We'd spend nights during the two-week waits after transfers doing comedy shows, impersonating friends, family and ex-partners all in a bid to smooth out some of the pain. We'd make light of the ridiculous comments and unwanted advice from anyone and everyone who made it their business. I remember the night we got pissed and devised a parody aptly named 'Infertility', with one scene including us setting fire to a batch of Monopoly money in the garden while imitating our infertility doctor telling us to *keep going*. I guess that's what I want to advise if you're reading this and still fighting. Arson. Just kidding. Laugh, *laugh* whenever you can and look for those moments even through great pain, because while you're still breathing, I promise you they are there. Only set fire to fake money, though; you're going to need to leave the real stuff for the clinics to burn through.

Back to the teeth whitening. I was full of it that day, not in the cocky, in love with oneself sense, just having an *all right day* vibe. I strutted right up to the young women on reception in their burgundy tunics announcing how I was here to have my teeth whitened, ensuring I was really showing off the specimens as I bestowed this information upon them. They weren't as enthused as I was, probably sick to the back teeth of people snarling their tea stains at them all day. As they checked me in, I eyed up the array of spa products I didn't need and wouldn't be able to afford after this blow-out but were available and, as I've touched upon, I'd developed a spectacular talent in trying to fulfil my unfulfilment by buying crap I did not need.

One of the girls gave me a questionnaire to complete. I asked if I could borrow a pen, which interrupted the nail varnish picking session she clearly needed to finish, so she offered a nod towards the pen pot. Once she'd completed her rustic manicure, I was led through the nicest smelling corridor I'd ever walked through; honestly, if you'd blindfolded me and said I was walking through a French lavender farm, I wouldn't have questioned it. Until she'd pushed opened the door and introduced me (sort of) in her strong West Country accent to the lady who would be responsible for my transformation.

There was a white, leather dentist's chair in the centre of the room. To the right of the door stood a coffee table and a less than inviting plastic chair. I decide to make myself comfortable on the chair of tooth whitening dreams while the tooth magician starts to rummage around for a colour chart. She's friendly, wearing a white tunic, and with an accent, could be Eastern European, Russian possibly. She asks a few pleasantries about me, before telling me about her two boys, which is all very nice, only I can't help but notice she has quite a few teeth missing. Now, I would be lying if I said this didn't cause concern for the welfare of my own. I mean by this stage I'm already in the chair; she's a very nice woman, but billboard for the brand and all that? She places the chart against my denticle, sliding it immediately towards the yellow shaded end. As she's doing this, she starts to explain how her pregnancies destroyed her teeth; she's clearly self-conscious given her profession and feels the need to explain her own denticulation.

She explains how the high levels of hormones in pregnancy caused tooth loosening and decay. I've never even heard of this before. I'm fascinated; she can tell I'm hooked in fact. I get the distinct impression she appreciates someone taking an interest and so offers up even more of her story, which I feel really rather honoured to hear. I remember thinking just how incredible women are as a species, the physical sacrifices they make to carry a child and the amazing strength of their bodies. Somewhere in between all of this we agree on the shade: white. Not Dulux ceiling white, just a nice sort of milky white. Once we've made the shade finalities, a large piece of plastic is inserted into my mouth and as she flicks the switch of the ultraviolet lamp on she asks me if I have kids.

I try to reply without dribbling.

'*No.*'

'*Don't bother*,' she says. Laughs and leaves the room.

I lie there like Wallace without his Gromit on an all-nighter. My mouth stretched horizontally open with only a fluorescent laser beam for company. I remember in that instance thinking how I desperately want to be a mum but also quite like having teeth.

Later, I would punish myself for that thought. There's a reason *why* people carry such vivid memories of certain life experiences, isn't there? Ones you could paint no matter how many years pass since, smells you're unable to forget, voices, faces, the colour of a wall, the feel of a fabric on your skin. Sensory triggers your brain just cannot eradicate.

Why?

Shock. You can't process disturbance in the moment, can you? Your brain has no choice but to live through it while taking a Polaroid picture, something to file in your long-term memory for later. Evidence that this day existed, it happened.

The stickiness of the white leather chair on the palms of my hands, the distinct smell of mouthwash mixed with vanilla air freshener and the voice and face of this woman is my Polaroid. Because it is this image that would be my very last moment on earth of being unaware I would no longer be able to try to conceive a child with the man I loved, without medical intervention.

I come strutting out of the dental salon bounding past the car park recycling bins like Pamela Anderson sprinting along Emerald Bay beach. I feel bloody spectacular and want my husband to receive nothing short of an Oscar nomination for his reaction to my new look. I fling open the car door and, lacking any elegance, slide onto the seat, pulling the passenger mirror down to get another peek at this newest member of Los Angeles County's lifeguards. This hopeful ego-fuelling session is swiftly interrupted by the ringing of one of our phones.

He sits in pained tranquillity.

I in tormented disbelief.

Fixated on the windscreen.

Watching the wipers sway left to right as a dribble of rain starts to escape from the sky.

I don't say anything.

The windscreen is slowly engulfed in a thick duvet of condensation. When it has fully disguised us, we feel secure enough to speak.

'*We won't be able to have kids, naturally,*' whispers the waffle.

'*We might not be able to have children, at all,*' replies the spaghetti.

I want to say how I lovingly threw my arms round his neck; I would have preferred to see myself respond like that. Instead, I completed the entire cycle of anger in about four minutes. After a short period of stunned silence, I'm demanding who the hell it was that deemed it appropriate to drop this bombshell over the phone in a car park. It wasn't even our designated GP who delivered the news; he was off sunning himself somewhere. *Yes*, everyone's entitled to a holiday. *No*, not when he's supposed to be delivering our test results. I didn't for one second think they'd got it wrong or our paperwork had been muddled up with the poor couple who couldn't really conceive, nothing like that. Call me old-fashioned but I like to get to know someone before I crush their hopes and dreams. It's painful enough hearing it from a medical professional you've built a bit of rapport with, let alone a duty doctor who had to check she'd even got our names right.

In among me flailing around some *what the hell happens now?* (along with other actual expletives) and *what are we going to do?* my husband reminds me that the doctor did specify she would need to find out what the next steps were and call us back. *Wonderful*. Didn't she think it might have been a good idea to come onto the phone *with* the 'next steps'? I think this is disgusting, absolute patient negligence. Is even a virtual bedside manner no longer a thing these days? I want her back on the phone with immediate effect. The phone rings; after giving it the Barry big licks for the past however many minutes, I crap myself and signal for my husband to start talking.

She's on speaker, seems like a very nice woman. Calm. Logical. I feel embarrassed now, so try to act equally as grounded, which doesn't seem to have the same effect, leaving me doing a fantastic impersonation of Batman's arch-enemy, the Joker.

Totally. Unhinged.

In this precise moment, that's *exactly* what I am – hanging on, without hinges.

She explains that we will be referred to our local treatment centre (no longer the GP's problem). Hopes of baby-making medicine by this point have been well and truly dashed. We're headlining the main stage now. Rollin' with the big boys. Official members of the one in seven club.

I watch the uninvited rain burst down onto the windscreen, the wipers frantically trying to clear the glass ahead of me. I'm jealous of the rain. I desperately want to burst into tears; I wish my initial reaction had been to cry. All my brain is consumed by is thoughts of us never becoming parents. I'm engulfed by this sudden fear of not ever getting to see the pattern of a child's eyes, hear the rhythm of their breath, never feel the finger bones of a tiny hand in between my own. Never hear the softness of a child's voice calling me 'Mummy' or the delicacy of a soft cheek as I kiss them goodnight.

'Do you like my teeth?'

I run a bath that evening, sit in it for ages, watching my skin shrivel up. I imagine looking in the mirror in years to come, seeing a pruned-up face staring back at me. I see a woman with a story she didn't get the chance to write, the one about an unconditional love between a mother and her child.

I think about medical intervention, my perceived Frankenstein-ness of it all. I think about all the times we'd been on holiday, the country weekends away, all the sickeningly picturesque settings we'd had to make our family, the times we'd made love then convinced ourselves that was 'the one'. Me, nestled in under his shoulder spending the rest of the weekend holding hands imagining we were creating life inside of me, just the two of us. Then I think about lying on the crispy white sheets of a hospital bed, exposing my eyes to the artificial spaceship lights above, legs in stirrups, a room full of strangers for company, and I feel really rather angry.

I put my head under the water, try to drown out the

reality of what's about to happen. I still can't cry, *why haven't I cried yet?* I get out of the bath, sit on my bed wrapped in a mustard-coloured towel for what must have been hours. Just sitting there. In silence. I try to moisturise, but I give up once I've reached my knees, what's the point? (Ironically, there's more point now than ever to keep the old knees spruced up, as half the medical team at the clinic would be chatting to them regularly.)

There's just enough time during this bath for my good old friend 'intrusive thought' to make an appearance: *Is this happening because you said you wanted to keep your teeth?*

I call my dad; I tell him nothing immediately of the diagnosis and why this is happening, only that I don't think I can do it. I don't want to step onto the merry-go-round of infertility treatment. Because I knew, I just knew, given our grade A competitive personality types, we wouldn't be able to get off. You're talking about a man who exercises six days a week and just doesn't seem to age and a woman who once timed herself hanging out her washing, *for fun*. I feel sick at the prospect of dedicating however many years of our lives to science and potentially having to walk away physically and financially empty handed. I wasn't all that clued-up on the world of infertility and its treatments but what I had heard of it was that it offered no guarantee, and it didn't come cheap.

He's the epitome of calm, my dad. Not one to raise his voice, I've never really seen him get all that flustered and not a lot shocks him. I've rung him on multiple occasions throughout my life in highly emotional states and never been able to catch him out. He's not the person if you're in search of a big reaction from an impromptu tattoo or partner choice. He's always just taken a back seat view and never really interfered, apart from that one time I accepted a marriage proposal on a Spanish island at the age of eighteen – I mean it was never going to actually *happen*, but he did have a few words to say about that. I used to question whether this was the approach of a parent who felt he had no right to an opinion because of his alcoholism. As though he'd relinquished his right to give us his thoughts because of his addiction, and I do still feel there could be some truth in that. But as we've grown together through my later years of childhood to now, I've realised that he's also just a decent human being who respects people's right of choice including his children's. He might ask you if *you* think you're doing the right thing, but he won't *tell you*. So, when I ring him to declare I don't care what they advise or offer us, I won't be doing it, he responds with:

'This is how you feel today. Maybe you just need to let it all play out in front of you. Listening to the facts, hearing what it is they have to say will allow that.'

He tells me *'to try not to worry'*. (He always says this to me, when I've watched too much *News at Ten* and I'm freaking out about a certain world leader pressing a certain button or I think I'm dying because I've Googled headaches.)

He signs off with:

'*There are lots of ways to start a family.*'
And
'*You can't foresee what's about to happen, but it will all work itself out.*' (Another Dad phrase which sometimes I like and at others I find really bloody unhelpful, a nothing phrase like 'what will be will be'. Who came up with that? Talk about reiterating the ambiguous.)

Then he tells me he's proud of me and he loves me.
Now I can cry.

He'd hit a nerve with his subliminal parenting style and idioms. Maybe in this immediate instant I didn't want any part of it, but did I want to risk a lifetime of wondering what might have played out? Knowing that I didn't even give the doctors a chance to tell me what the options were, an opportunity to discuss or explore possibilities and it's not just about me, is it? I mean, there are two individuals very much involved here. Two people who fell in love and wanted to have a family, who stood up together in a wooden beamed building full of friends and family promising to support each other in sickness and in health. So far, all I'd managed to do was make it all about myself. Isolate myself in the bathroom then the bedroom for most of the evening. We'd both had this news, me and the person I was closer to than anyone else in the world, yet I just needed to be on my own. I wish I could be better, more selfless, but I couldn't cope with much more than myself. Besides, that's what I did when faced with the familiar feeling of rejection and abandonment – dusted off the old exoskeleton, that hard exterior shell, turned my back on those who cared, kicking a protective veil of dust behind me with my hind legs, like the angry cockroach I still was.

I get off the phone.

My dad's words etched into my brain.

I stand up to take a cold, hard look at myself in the mirror.

My nose is just a few millimetres away from the glass. I look at my eyes, the colour, the shape, I look at my eyelashes, the freckle on my nose, the genetic chip (passed down from my dad) in my front, left, newly whitened tooth. I feel burning salty tears making their way down my chin. I stuff a pillow in my mouth, curl up into a ball.

And. Scream.

Que Sera, Sera.

Fish Tanks

There's always a fish tank in these sorts of places. I can guarantee you at least one infertility consultation will involve you having to sit next to a fish tank. They're relaxing, aren't they? The bubbles, lights, the way the fish move with such effortless elegance through the water. A slightly insensitive interior choice perhaps, considering fish can lay up to a thousand eggs a year. I'm sitting by the tank, my husband's taking advantage of the free coffee. He can't stomach the stuff usually but has no issues digesting a freebie so he's happily filling up one of those eco-friendly cups like there's no tomorrow. Talking of freebies, that subject is definitely on the top of our questions agenda today.

We're sitting directly opposite two other couples. That's another thing these places seem to do, arrange the seating in such a way that it makes it nigh on impossible to avoid eye contact with other infertility passengers. One woman has affectionately interlocked her arm into her partner's. He's flicking through some sort of glossy brochure on his lap; she's practically leaning over his face to see what it is that's caught his attention (probably a subtotal of the financial collateral damage). They still look hopeful, though, excited, in love.

To the left of Walt and Disney there's a woman with a clipboard resting on her knees, filling out some paperwork. Every so often she offers out a thoughtful pause to the universe, puts her pen to her lips and looks across to her partner who's extremely busy on his phone. (Looking a bit more familiar with the process and slightly less hopeful, these two.) Now, I'm no infertility detective, but I would hazard a guess that on the right we have a couple of first timers and to the left a couple of experienced cycle-ists. We, on the other hand, are sort of somewhere in the middle: by no means full of the joys of spring but still talking to each other.

Behind our new friends I can see some double doors and above them the sign reads: *Recovery Ward*, and to the right of these doors: *Theatre*. A nurse eccentrically bursts out from between the recovery ward doors; she's smiling, saying hello to everyone. She's wearing blue scrubs and matching shower cap. She's friendly, all the staff are, only there's one thing no amount of smiling can eradicate: how strikingly clinical everything is. Take away the fish tanks, coffee machines and strategically placed chairs and you're left with consultation rooms, an operating theatre, recovery ward and a good half a dozen people feeling pretty down in the fertility dumps.

There are posters neatly plastered all over the walls,

detailing support groups on offer, contact details of therapists, dates of information evenings, then there's the really interesting section, the stats. The truth behind the scientific fate. This is, after all, what we're here to do; pass your procreation destiny over to the hands of medical science, but just *how successful* are the results of this science?

I'd *never* up until this point researched or even thought about stats. I'd read almost every horror story on every forum page on the internet but possessed not an ounce of rationality within me to look up some *facts*. Even if I had, I would have only gone straight to 'success rates', not to 'live birth rates' – why would I? I've just woken up on this bizarre planet after a pretty turbulent flight. I can't be expected to speak the bloody lingo right away. Yet there it was, clear for all those who wanted to see, on a poster stuck to a clean white wall.

Treatment success rates naturally took pride of place in a slighter larger, enticing (get me pregnant now) font and some way down below in a significantly smaller font, just above a picture of a smiling baby with bright blue eyes, *Live birth rates*. Actual babies born. Not the dream of a positive pregnancy test, but the birth of an actual child.

And those stats were very different.

The NHS reports that in 2019, 'IVF treatments that resulted in a live birth' were as follows:[2]

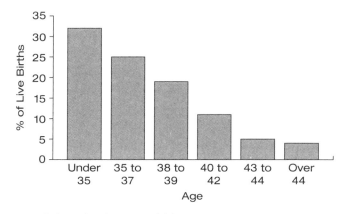

I didn't think it would be 100 per cent. I've never been that much of an optimist even at the best of times. In all honesty I don't really know what percentage I thought it might be, just higher than that. I can see my husband is looking at the stats having similar thoughts to mine: is this even worth it? Knowing our competitive characteristics and how tough this could get because instinctively you just know before you even begin that it's got the ability to eat you both up. We sit staring at this sheet of paper, hand in hand, him clutching his eco-friendly cup a little tighter than before, silently asking ourselves if we truly possess the strength within us to climb aboard the family-making slot machine.

A delighted squeal from the receptionist prevents us from falling into a momentary pit of depression. She jumps up from behind the desk to greet a couple beaming from ear to ear (which makes them stand out because, I can tell you, none of the rest of us are smiling). She appears to be talking to the guy's knees, making weird noises, frantically smiling (must be quite the set of knees). Mr Knees' wife steps to the side to reveal the car seat he's holding, the seat carrying a tiny baby who can be only a few weeks old.

He's been brought in to meet the people who enabled him to draw breath.

Suddenly the stats don't mean shite.

It comes down to one of two stats, really.

Hope.

No hope.

As we stand there staring at this tiny human in his trendy car seat, we hear our names called by a short, smiley man. He's kind; I'm met with his sincere sense of kindness almost immediately. He *wants* you to become a success stat. Two reasons why I came to this assumption of his character: one, the way he shook my hand. He carefully held my palm while wrapping the other delicately around the outside of my exposed skin, as if to stop it from feeling the cold. Two, the fifteen-minute-later look of utter discomfort on his face when he dropped the postcode lottery bombshell, followed by a price list.

In order for us to have even a percentage of a chance, we needed treatment. They call it cycles, only they have no idea exactly *how many* of these cycles it may take to get you pregnant, and now we know the aim here is not just to *get* pregnant, but to carry a full-term pregnancy and give birth. A cycle basically involves the female having to medically suppress her menstrual cycle, which can be done with a nasal spray or daily injections. She then takes a fertility hormone to help her produce more eggs before they are then collected under sedation, fertilised (hopefully) and transferred into the womb (hopefully). That's the professional, sensible, scientific explanation. Now, I'll share with you how it translated in my head: 'You're going to need to suppress your period, which is probably going to turn you into an absolute psychopath because let's be real. You will threaten to divorce your husband and take the nicer of the two sofas *at least* once throughout that glorious seven-day period at the best of times, before they knock you out on an operating table while they rummage round your nether regions on some dodgy Easter egg hunt extracting whatever they can get their hands on followed by a bit of sperm meet egg bribery before the *pièce de résistance*: shoving it all back inside via a catheter, in order for you to pee on a stick a few weeks later with a high probability of two v's up on the old Clear Blue (other tests widely available). Of course, you *could* get lucky, strike it hot first time round, waltz out of here wiping away your tears of happiness on one of those fifty-pound notes you didn't have to spend.'

God, I sound bitter. Look, I've got nothing against the treatment. Honestly. I think fertility treatment, when it works, has got to be one of medicine's greatest gifts. It's given hope and opportunity to many people to whom it would otherwise have been denied. My issue sits with the profits made, the exploitation and lack of regulation of it all.

Only very recently a BBC analysis showed how 41

per cent of clinics offering women egg freezing services privately could be breaching advertising guidance set by Watchdog which clearly states; 'clinics must not give false or misleading information'.

They discovered thirty-two websites were not transparent with the chances of successfully having a baby. And of that group, most of these sites were publishing successful thaw rates. Another misleading example of clinics cherry-picking information and tactfully failing to highlight the difference between egg survival and live birth rates.[3]

I sit there, listening to all the medical jargon, offer the odd nod, an attempt at looking mildly intellectual. I try to process the need to inject myself into forcibly producing more eggs, so they can retrieve the eggs, then put one back in. Seems like a hell of a lot of effort.

He eventually stops talking infertility NASA and starts talking cash. Suddenly my IQ level picks up. He explains how we're entitled to *one* free cycle of treatment on the NHS and that decision has been made because funding amounts are subject to postcode areas and our six-digit code falls into the bracket of one free cycle. He looks genuinely upset as he shares this with us. He's only too aware of the inequality within the system and it saddens him, I can see that. Now readers, look, I know we're exceptionally lucky, anyone living in the UK with access to a service as incredible as the NHS is plain lucky, that's just a fact. In that respect there really is so much to be grateful for, but there's also a significant difference between not having gratitude and a recognition of plain discrimination. I knew of a woman who lived no more than thirty minutes from us, and she'd been very open about her IVF journey and the *three* funded cycles she had been entitled to. We're talking thirty minutes up the road, not a sail and rail across the emerald sea.

I start to peel the blue coating from one corner of the clipboard attaching more forms I'd been asked to complete. I hear my husband ask with a light but most definite tone of panic, '*What happens if it doesn't work? What options do we have then?*' The kind doctor slides a brochure across the table; there's nothing slick about the manoeuvre, it's uncomfortable. He signals us to flick through the therapeutically coloured pale greys and tranquil blues cycle package brochure, featuring a picture of a baby in a nappy and the face of the mother looking utterly content.

I've worked in sales, I've trained people how to source, negotiate and clinch the deal, sat on brand design meetings. So, I'm very aware that every marketing campaign, advert, billboard and brochure needs a target customer and I feel quite sick knowing that *we* are the target customers of this particular brochure. One featuring the potential promise of a human life.

In the space of about sixty minutes, I'd already decided I didn't like this new world, not any part of it from the marketing, choice words, payment plans, rose-tinted spectacle stats, inequalities, any physical part of the process or the sales pitch. I really didn't like it at all.

When I reflect on my journey to motherhood, I've

always felt as though we *fell* into the world of infertility treatment. As if we opened the door to our GP's office with no security of any floorboards underneath and just fell through a big black hole, landing with a thump on the egg retrieval floor. I definitely didn't allow my brain enough time to process or accept our diagnosis and what that truly meant before I started using my stomach as a pin cushion for the foreseeable. One minute I'm confiding in my GP, next there's some woman in a shower cap inserting a blastocyst via a catheter, announcing how the *'entire team working at the clinic wish you the very best of luck'*. You've taken off on the baby-making rollercoaster before anyone's even come round to check you're wearing a seat belt.

Interestingly, before you can even submit a Registration of Interest to adopt in the UK, you are required to take a significant break from any previous route to parenthood efforts before you can proceed any further. My understanding is that this aims to protect your mental health and well-being, but paramount to any of that is the protection of the child you may be matched with. To give you the time and rational understanding of exactly what it is you're about to embark on, to really ensure you have allowed yourself time to grieve for what it is you have lost, because infertility is a loss and adoption is certainly not a replacement for any lost biological hopes and dreams. The honoured opportunity of adopting a child is a very separate hope and dream. Adoption agencies need to know you're fully committed to the process and to the children waiting. Bloody good on them for that, I say.

I'd better expand on what a match is. Once you've been approved to adopt, you then need to be matched with a child or children, ensuring your skills and life experience can match with their needs. This is then formally agreed at a matching panel at the child's local authority.

When people ask *why* you can't start both treatment and the adoption process side by side, I like to remind them that if you want to play hook a duck with yourself that's fine, but this isn't the county fair, it's not about how many strikes you can line up before you 'get lucky'. It's about making a very clear-cut, ethical decision as an adult about committing to a process designed in only the best interests of the children who would quite like to stop spinning around. I would advise not wasting the system's dangerously stretched financial resources if you're questioning this commitment. The impact of any uncertainty only truly impacts the most vulnerable.

The level of care taken in the adoption process begs a question of the fertility industry. From a duty of care perspective, should there be a more supportive approach for infertility patients from the day they leave their GP's office? Should individuals' emotional needs and capabilities be assessed in a supportive and informed environment prior to handing their baby-making fate over to the hands of the science Gods? There's a whole world of difference between starting a family the tried and tested way and that of involving science.

Of course, I'm not talking about denying people treatment. I'm suggesting greater honesty and emotional guidance. In my opinion (which is the only one I can have), more of an independent, impartial bridge between the GP's office and the fertility clinic is needed, providing an opportunity to explore all avenues or even linger a while. But then, that would disrupt the substantial profits of this thriving commercial business model, wouldn't it? Organic fish food doesn't come cheap. I can't imagine these clinic fish are surviving on your basic flakes. The GP advises only on the treatment options, feeding directly into the clinic; the clinics profit from the hyper-inflated prices of a simple blood test alone; and then, filling their boots right at the very end, we have the pharmaceutical companies rolling in the begged, borrowed and hard-earned cash from those desperate for a family.

I don't have the answer or any right to promote one, but having sat in that requested period of pause I can say it was only really during that time that I could grieve and scrape enough of myself together to reach the epiphany of what it really was that I'd wanted in the first place. To *love* a child. Motherhood.

It was living through a period of nothingness that enabled me to make without question the best decision of my entire life.

This isn't a public declaration of regretting treatment or the feeling of guilt creeping in for ever doing it – a guilt I believe many adoptive parents face – but any shame or guilt must be left at the door. We all have a story, we're all on a voyage, remember. You won't ever reach the ending destined for you unless you climb aboard. I don't regret; I just wish I'd known there is *great* love to be found in unexpected places, that we needn't always only look under the rocks we're herded towards turning over.

The kind doctor has a smaller fish tank in his office, a significant downgrade from that of the waiting room. He's still got a few decent-looking fish in there and one of those colour changing filters. While I'm counting the seconds between each colour change, I hear him offer the answer to my husband's question, '*What if it doesn't work at all?*'

It's forty-five, a strong forty-five seconds between each filter colour change. The doctor starts to talk about donor conception, a process potentially enabling us to have a child that would bear 50 per cent of our genetics. An alternative path to parenthood that has enabled thousands to become parents. An incredible opportunity for many but didn't feel like the right fit for us. We needed only a relatively short discussion about this option after our appointment. This discussion was the very first probe towards thinking about genetics and the possibility of relinquishing them. What came out of this, for us, was the reflective questioning of there even being an importance to genetics at all.

Astoundingly, this was a thought that had never been

put to me for consideration before. Not at school, by the media, *Question Time*, over a coffee. Not once had the topic of genetic importance and motherhood cropped up. I'd never heard anyone drill down on what it could be that really made a family, and that just seems utterly absurd, sitting here now, thinking about it.

While I'm in no position to advise, if you are faced with a similar decision, I think it's partly about asking yourself how much this *matters to you*. This is an elephant of a question with many different avenues to explore, such as is it the continuation of generational genetics? Or, seeing bits of your partner in your child in the physical sense? Because what seems insignificant to some can feel overwhelmingly important to others.

During our trip to the fertility aquarium, one family planning method that was never mentioned, among all the talk of cycles, donor conception, even childlessness, was adoption.

The prospect of a child who I would not carry, give birth to or either one of us share a genetic relationship with never got a mention. Why? I still don't know. Well, I mean we know why it's not mentioned in these places really, but if doctors are introducing family planning methods you hadn't anticipated anyway – like donors and surrogacy – *why* isn't the prospect of adoption mentioned along with all the others? If those cards-on-the-table conversations need to happen before treatments begin, it's not really a wholly informative conversation, is it?

There's an urban myth still circulating that places adoption in a league table of choices. How many times will a heterosexual couple, having become parents through adoption, be asked if they couldn't have 'their own' children?

Not one part of that question is OK; in fact, near enough every word of it is wildly insensitive. (They *are* their 'own children', for starters, and it's really none of your damn business.) This archaic assumption is that you adopt only if you couldn't conceive children.

Well, *Extra! Extra! Read all about it!*

There are actual, living people out there who have *only ever* considered adoption as the way to create their family; then there are people like me, who made the choice to try treatment and then the choice to adopt, and it happened in that order because that's just how it happened. Adoption is still a choice, the most considered, beautiful one I ever made in my life. Assumptions about that choice only singe the truth. No one has ever dragged a prospective adopter to an open information evening and filled out the paperwork for them. (You'd never find anyone willing to complete that amount of paperwork for a start.) Some arrive at its door after one round of infertility treatment, none or ten. Either way, they arrive, and they've done so because they've made the decision to do something:

Love.

And it really doesn't matter in what order you have this epiphany.

I just hope you have it because it really can be beautiful.

We leave the clinic and its selection of marine life behind, my handbag full of memorabilia, price lists and glossy brochures; I've even stolen a pen. I had my eye on a fish but there wasn't a huge amount of room in the car for the tank. We head home as a family of two still trying to decipher if we'll ever make it to three with the offer of one free cycle on the table – which we both know damn well we're going to take because free has never been a swear word in this relationship – our minds whirring with remnants of conversations we'd never had, until today.

Mules, Mannequins and Gin

'Hi. This is going to sound odd, but I'm having some drugs delivered. I was wondering if you could store them in your fridge for me?'

Alongside starting your first round of injections, inexplicable crying and intermittent bickering sessions with your partner, you also acquire a new hobby: losing any kind of privacy whatsoever. It wouldn't matter if you'd had previous work experience with MI5, it is virtually *impossible* to keep your infertility treatment a secret from anyone, including your lesser-acquainted friends or neighbours. If you don't find yourself needing to just offer up personal information for drug storage purposes, there's likely to be some who take it upon themselves to remind you during the festive period how magical children make Christmas before asking just why it is you don't want a sprinkling of said wizardry. Some people will always deem it OK to continue probing into *why* a couple don't have children. Trying to divert the interrogation through the medium of humour won't work either; they usually don't have a sense of one for a start, and if they do it's likely to lack any sensitivity. Unfortunately, people and their vulgar need to know will just catch you off-guard from time to time, and whatever your reaction may be to that (providing it's not physically aggressive) is absolutely fine.

Interestingly enough, the mules next door didn't ask a thing about my drug storage request, only what temperature they had to be stored at (sign of a professional). I knew the delivery was arriving at some point that day but had no fixed time. I had to get to work then straight to a party like the social butterfly I was and remembered reading that the drugs had to be kept chilled. If I was going to inject the stuff, I may as well follow the instructions – don't want to sprout an extra tail or anything. I wasted no time at all in marching over to knock on my neighbour's door requesting if she would harbour the goods in my absence. After her immediate, no-strings-attached agreement to the deal, she made just one passing comment:

'*I hope you're both OK.*'

I can't tell you just how bloody refreshing that was.

There's this odd thing that starts to happen when a couple can't conceive. It's the intrinsic need other people develop to make it all about them. Questions deemed acceptable to ask just to quench their own curiosity, decisions made claiming to have your best interests at heart when really it's because it makes things easier for them. Take pregnancy announcements as an example. As soon as there's a whiff of someone struggling with infertility, people start to think it's contagious. Speakeasy-style baby showers start popping off all over the shop, only you're not to be granted the entry password. Newborns snuggled in prams are swiftly diverted to the other side of the road as soon as you're within communicable distance. It's a damn complicated one, this; we need someone really smart to come along and try to solve this piece of social algebra because it really is an equation and a half. I was so unspeakably hurt when I *wasn't* invited or was bypassed, but by the same token, I *didn't want* to be asked or seen. So, you tell me, gang. What's the solution to the friendship assassinator that is infertility?

The only pearls of wisdom I have to offer up: Be more mule. *Don't. Make. It. About. You.* I'm not saying that our friends, acquaintances and significant others weren't devastated for us, heartbroken in fact, and, in the immediate moments, people are there, wanting to hear your plan of action, advising you as best they can. Offering to attend appointments, showering you with the finest bath bombs, scented candles and chocolate orange buttons. Turning up with bottles of wine suggesting we try and numb the pain away for an evening.

Only it's emotionally taxing, isn't it? Listening to the same old shit, week after week, month after month, year after year. Radiators and drains, as my husband's nan used to say: '*In life, you've got radiators and drains, no one wants to hang around the drains for too long.*'

That's the bottom line here: none of them expected it to bore on for so long. I think what people don't anticipate is having to wait in the wings on emotional standby *years* after the initial diagnosis. Friendship is a two-way thing, give and take and all that. Only you can't give when you're trying to survive, you can't be that pillar of support during a friend's pregnancy when you're scuttling around without your head, and I think it takes an incredible amount of selflessness from a friend to truly understand and accept that.

I'll confess I came out of this a bit of a Billy No-Mates. Not even a bit, just a Billy. With no mates. Infertility can do that, and if that's to be your story too, you're going to be just fine.

That's a cockroach promise.

Eventually I was met with no choice but to come clean to my boss. There's only so many times a car can break down without your employer suggesting you skateboard to work, and I couldn't find my way out of a paper bag without a Sat Nav so it was never going to be a viable solution. It was time to confess. I hadn't not told work because I was embarrassed or ashamed of the situation; I hadn't mentioned it because I was worried. I might not get a pay rise, or a new swivel chair for my dedication to the company, and in all honesty, I didn't see *why* I should damn well have to. No one trying to get pregnant naturally has to announce it over a networking lunch. Not one person has to announce their marital antics during AOB. They're just getting on with it (literally) and the office is none the wiser. When you're not in the 84 per cent, however, you're at risk of going in to work on a Monday, requesting Wednesday off for egg collection and by Tuesday every one of your colleagues has been well and truly informed your eggs are soon to be leaving the building. Infertility, the silent condition that strips you of any career progression or pay rise before skipping off with your privacy.

Right, where were we? Oh yes, asking my neighbour to stash drugs next to her bolognaise. While the drugs were on ice down at fairy-tale way, we were on our way to a party. Alcohol was strictly off the menu for me these days, so I wasn't expecting it to be the most eventful evening; evenings never are when there are no cocktails involved, and you're forced to recognise exactly who it is you're talking to and take accountability for what you're saying. I refer to nights like this as Refined Socialisation and actually I needed to go. In recent months I had been struggling to socialise; I'd noticed myself becoming more and more introverted. Making it through the working week really was taxing enough without having to attend any extra-curricular activities. However, I was aware of the social thinning that had been appearing around us of late so was determined to make a conscious effort to show my face, even if it wasn't the most approachable.

We arrive within our usual timeframe – late. I make it through the front door, politely pushing my way through a hallway of aftershave and perfume scents, into the kitchen where I conduct a full assessment of the surroundings, surveying where I can position myself, looking for a spot that doesn't quite shout *don't approach me.* I'm aiming for an air of *I really am very happy over here with the Twiglets. Please don't feel the need to introduce yourself* and would you believe it, I find just the spot.

I do love a Twiglet and think they get a lot of bad press. Granted they aren't the most attractive-looking snack, resembling a pair of knobbly old knees sporting a pair of wartime brown tights, but if you've got the capability to look beyond that, they really are the perfect crunchy party snack. They're also made from wholewheat flour, making them high in fibre. Which means they're good for you, giving you licence to eat the whole bowl.

There I am, halfway through a ceramic dish of knobbly, tight-wearing knees, when I'm approached by a woman who clearly hasn't got the intended message. Her wildly expressive '*Hi!*' grants me the displeasure of inhaling the alcohol from her breath, and judging by the fact I can practically taste the gin and tonic she's so selflessly sharing, I assume she's having a damn good night. We exchange pleasantries, asking how we both know the host before she releases a hugely animated sigh, widening her mouth much like a hippo, her warning to me that *she* will be asserting complete control of our conversation, before announcing how she and her husband have been trying to start a family for a few months and nothing has happened yet.

I've never bitten into a pair of knobbly knees harder in all my life.

I'm understandably flabbergasted by this stranger who has unnecessarily offered up such intimate details of her private life after a total conversation of about fifteen words. She's also rather uncomfortably just standing there staring at me, before requesting a solution to her predicament: '*What do* you *think we should do?*' Now, I'm no Miss Marple but I'm going to have to hazard a guess that the only reasoning behind this svelte hippopotamus deeming me the on-site infertility specialist would be down to the mutual friend I had confided in about starting treatment. She clearly hadn't filed this as confidential information, instead granting herself permission to distribute it among her nearest and dearest. Although I couldn't be 100 per cent sure and of course it could also just be a massively wild coincidence. Mercifully, the hippo is thirsty and in need of a top-up, which I'm only too understanding of – they actually need up to 56 gallons a day – so off she locomotes towards the nearest gin-filled lake.

I need to think on my trotters here and relocate, sharpish. That's more than enough socialising for one night. I spy my husband through the crack of the lounge door and take it upon myself to swoop in and rescue him from the conversation he's actually enjoying. He flashes me the 'everything OK?' look. When you're married to an introverted extrovert (also known as ambivert) you know only too well that your spouse could be dancing on top of the table one minute and sitting under it with a *do not disturb* sign the next. Before I can answer, she's back! Galloping through, her webbed feet barely touching the ground like an aquatic hippo ballet dancer. This hungry hippo is on the hunt for more high fibre snacks and infertility insights; she's taking definite strides towards me. This time she's moving in a bloat, bringing company in the form of a partner hippo. They seem friendly enough, offering a hand out to both me and my husband. Among all this look-giving and hand-shaking, a good four or five other spectators enter the room. Hippos enjoy resting in cool water, observing, heads only partially submerged, leaving their tiny ears, beady eyes and flared nostrils protruding from the water, allowing them not to miss a trick. Nosey gits.

She starts to cry uncontrollably about the prospect of not being able to get pregnant, which of course I have empathy for. I'm about to try to comfort her by sharing how a few months of trying naturally in the world of procreation science is considered really very early days, but I can't because she starts aggressively whispering (they do get angry, hippos) about how they could end up like me and my husband, trying for ages and needing treatment.

At this point, my husband and I are just standing there, like a couple of mannequins on full display, pride of place in a shop window. Merely representations of the human form, considered lacking in any actual feelings. Her partner tries to respond but efforts are drowned out by her now shouting across the room the exact reason why we can't have children.

The mannequins are left to stand there, exposed for all to see, stripped of their clothes and any right to individual privacy like a couple of party pieces, wheeled out for the evening's entertainment. Bashfully they shuffle their way past the audience, back through the hallway of fumes and into their car where they hold the flesh of each other's hands, flesh that had not been seen, and release the tears people thought they didn't have.

I will be honest in sharing the fact that my friendship with the host never survived that night. I tried for years afterwards but I could never shake off the hurt of it all. My personal failing – because it usually takes two to contribute towards any relationship breakdown – was simply not being honest enough. Making out that evening's events hadn't cut as deep as they had. I stayed quiet and suppressed the truth because I didn't know how to handle the situation – who does really? This relationship didn't fully break down during our years of treatment, but instead after we had finished, when I felt strong enough to speak the truth. I suppose by then it was too late. I'd already let it fester and had a little black book of petty things that had ticked me right off. Of course, the crux of it all was the mannequins. On reflection, had I found the strength, I should have faced into it at the time, head on. Maybe our friendship would have survived, who knows. Hindsight's an interesting thing.

Infertility is hugely socially disruptive, 'the friendship assassin'. Not many know how to handle it, not friends, family or the ones trying to survive it. Having come scuttling through the ruins with only one set of wings less than I went in with, I can say hand on heart I don't believe there was ever malice in things that were said. Really, I don't. There needed to be more boundaries around what was shared, but in terms of malice, I believe there was not an ounce. That's what makes it all so tragic.

I was guilty in many ways, I suppose, making out I could cope, trying so hard to be a version of my pre-infertility self. I gave Academy Award-worthy performances of being nothing but happy for friends sharing their pregnancy news, desperate not to rain on their baby-making parade. I was *infertility masking* – it's a new term I've invented, something you do when you try to hold onto your friends. I was hiding and disguising parts of myself in order to fit in with the rest of the room. Only it didn't work, never does when you're not being true to yourself. It always comes out in the wash, as they say, and do you know what still breaks my heart even now? Deep, deep down I was genuinely happy for others, but even deeper down, right at the very core, I was dying. I fought too hard to prevent anyone seeing that. The public façade I put on for fear of being labelled the world's biggest party pooper was totally and utterly exhausting.

I hope this book will be one that friends of those struggling to reach parenthood will read and it's because of this hope that I want to share how, even if your friend makes it through this time in their life, they won't come out the other side unscathed. That's what infertility does in my experience: it alters you, and usually during a time of life where your friend will have to sit on the side-lines and wave everyone off onto the pitch they too wanted to be playing on. If you love your friend, keep throwing them the ball;

they might chuck it back differently but it's still the same pair of hands.

There is no behavioural manual for those immediately impacted, or the network around them, when it comes to the meteoroid that is infertility. What do I hope we could all get better at? Respecting boundaries. Boundaries around the language that's used, the questions that are asked and the strict confidence in which personal information is shared. How do we go ahead and enforce these boundaries? Well, it's usually after something has gone wrong, after we've learnt from our mistakes, lost friendships and started putting up fireguards after we've all got burnt. Mannequins can melt, you know.

Have respect and, if you can, be more honest than me.

The Perfect Stranger

I'd once, *maybe* twice, felt the need for a mother figure in my life since mine left. I'd never really looked to fill that void with a female friendship or feminine guidance; in fact, I was quite good at repelling relationships with females in general, and if I did manage to form one, I'd usually find a way to wriggle out of it a few years down the line when it started to become uncomfortably familiar. I've never gone out searching for a dependable female to help me through the trials and tribulations of life, so it's a remarkable turn of events that the maternal nurturing and love that I didn't even recognise I was wanting found its way to me as a grown woman during one of the most difficult stages in my adult life.

I walk into a puppy training class. Lord knows my little white, extremely high-spirited, no-discipline-whatsoever Maltese terrier needs it. He arrives in his usual style of barking and snarling at every dog there, so the instructor directs us both to a seat right at the very back, away from pretty much every other man or beast – damage limitation. I'm pretty sure she would have had us participate from the external side of the window if she could have got away with it. In walks this absolutely *beautiful* woman. She's quite a bit older than me, which makes her even more beautiful, at a guess early sixties. Her dog, playing up to the stereotype of looking like their owners, is prancing in like something off the Milan doggy catwalk. Her fluffy black pooch seems to have taken quite a shine to my little reprobate and he to her. The beautiful lady smiles at me and offers a soft '*Hello*' while opening a bag of dog treats and asking if it would be OK to give one to the '*love dogs*', affectionately laughing as they lick each other's noses. I can detect the possibility of a slight Northern accent. I can't get over how nice they smell, her and the dog; it's like the entire fragrance floor of a department store has just burst through the doors in search of some behavioural pointers. Her clothes look really soft and well loved, she's effervescent, sprightly, full of life and there's a mischievous look to her bluey-green eyes.

We spend most of the class together laughing at the fact our dogs only have an interest in snogging one another when they really ought to, at the very least, be attempting a 'sit'. We leave the class, walking past her car. I'm struggling to find my keys in the never-ending pit of my leather backpack, which isn't an unusual ritual, and my bronzer escapes, cracking all over the pavement in front of us. She starts to giggle, suggests trying to pick it all up and glue it back together, which is a ridiculous suggestion, but the naughty way in which she delivers the idea means

I can't help but go along with it. I start pretending to pick up grains of powder from the floor while she asks for my mobile number for fears her dog may have fallen head over heels for mine and she really won't know how to break it to her later if she won't be able to send him a goodnight text.

A week or so after texting sweet nothings on behalf of our dogs, we meet in a café. I don't remember a huge amount of what we discussed over my flat white and her hot chocolate, only that she called me '*A beautiful girl*'. She says it more than once, maybe two or three times, each time with a smile, and although I have absolutely no idea what the hell is going on and would usually shut down any compliments quicker than my husband goes round switching all the lights off after me, I actually quite like it. There's a woman, older than me, saying something nice and it really doesn't appear that she is going to change her mind or try to steal those things away by reminding me of my larger than average nose or how you needed to be pretty and thin to become a dancer. *This* woman is just going to let me have it, the compliment, and I, for the first time in an achingly long age, am going to allow someone to give it to me.

She won't know this, my lovely friend – not unless she reads this book – but I cried that evening, just a little bit. Had a cheeky little look in the bathroom mirror and smiled.

There can be great healing power from strands of love gifted from a stranger. I believe in strands of love and the evolving capabilities in which someone might be ready to accept some. For me, there was the part of the brain that had survived the act of ending up in care, then there was the part still trying to process the *why* and the tragedy of it having to play out that way, and will probably do so for the rest of my life. The way in which a care leaver, like me, freezes every time a bank or utilities company asks for my mother's maiden name over the phone. I find that question hugely triggering and a somewhat archaic security approach in terms of reflecting and including the variety of family units we have today.

Don't even get me started on *next of kin*.

Who do our young adults of the care system put down as a person to contact in an emergency at fifteen or sixteen years old when they simply don't have anyone reliable or functioning enough at home? What name do they give when their assigned social worker changes like the wind? Kin by definition means *one's family or relations*. What if you don't want to name some stranger you've only been living with for a few months? Why should you have to, if you deem them neither a friend nor a relation? Another thing is asking young job applicants how many schools they've attended on an application form when, for some, the boxes provided just won't be enough. We're supposed to be living in the 'pro-social' era, right? To me, it feels as though we still have a whole load of pro-social work to do when it comes to reflecting anything other than the all-American, Sunny D-loving 2.4 with a white picket fence.

Take statutory adoption pay as an example. If you're

a self-employed parent to a biological child in the UK, you currently receive £172.48 a week in statutory maternity pay. If you're self-employed and adopting a child, however, you get nothing. I've been campaigning to change this act of discrimination for nearing two years now, taking a petition exceeding 16,000 signatures to parliament and securing a debate. You can watch said debate,[4] read the manuscript and the research, as well as what the public said via the UK Government and parliament petitions website/Hansard.[5] (If you do give any of this your time, lend your ear to the discriminatory truths shared from the public.)

An entire gallery of us sat in parliament on 21 March 2022 and listened to statements such as:

'The system was not actively designed to favour one set of parents over another. It is an anomaly.'

'More than 80,000 children are in care, a number which is at a record high. Anything that we can do to get permanence for those children must be to their benefit and to the benefit of society as a whole.'

'I really do not believe that the cost to the Exchequer would be very much, but the return on that investment in our children will be huge [. . .] I hope we can get the bureaucracy out of the way to give them just that.'

Many ministerial meetings two years on, I can exclusively reveal (hold on to your teeth) the bureaucracy is still very much in the way, as is this god-awful piece of discriminative legislation.

Hence the name; NOT A FICTIONAL MUM.

I digress (again).

But look, you get my gist, and a side-line to all this is that, although I'd survived my childhood, presenting as a well-functioning adult in a semi-detached with organised recycling bins, there will always be triggers. Be it suspicious energy providers or women being nice. More specifically, women significantly older than me. Either way, they were an uncomfortable reminder of a relationship I had been denied.

She was persistent, this perfect stranger. Messaging a few times a week, asking how I was. Making me laugh with pictures of her dog striking various poses sat next to love letters penned to mine. She was artistic, vibrant, full of love and positivity. In the moments we spent together I would enjoy her company but would always be left with a reflective suspicion. *Why* does this woman continue to reach out to me? What is her *agenda* exactly? *Why* is she so obstinately kind? Ending nearly every text with a compliment, whether it be about my career, image or personality, she was always so nice. Unusually for me, I awkwardly embraced it all but remained familiarly guarded. I'd tried to ask myself what she could possibly want from me. But I really couldn't think of a lot. *Maybe, she just likes you,* I would tell my sceptical self. Over the next few months, I started to relax into the maternal female company, looking forward to our dog walks and coffee dates, me confiding in her about our infertility, her delivering batches of insanely delicious homemade soups, consistently checking in on me even when I'd been unable to return the kindness.

One day she confides in me.

She tells me how she lost her daughter.

She speaks with great love and a magnitude of pain about the little girl who lived for just an hour and thirty minutes.

In that moment, I'm struck by the painful but very real complexity of there being mothers without their children. Without their child to hold or bring home, but who are *still* and always will be mothers to those children. That mothers after loss, be it from death or estrangement, can love deeply from the greatest distance. The bravery of her heartache humbles me, a lot. I think her and her daughter really very wonderful.

Many years later my perfect stranger was asked by someone at a party if she was my mum.

She replied:

'*I wish I was.*'

I only hope I'm asked the same question about her one day so I can borrow her answer.

Someone who should have loved me better once told me I would spend the rest of my life motherless. Whilst they were right in the literal, adjective sense, what can never be predicted is who we come to meet in life and who it is we find welcoming us into their lives.

The beauty of that relationship has been the way in which we both *chose* to love.

The most empowering part being my eventual ability to accept.

African Elephants and a Hot Pink Brush

What this book can't be is an account of events detailing our entire infertility journey. Partly because I don't have the patience or creative ability to make it interesting and, as feared, we didn't jump off after the one free cycle. Treatment took centre stage in my life for far too long, so I'll be damned if I end up dedicating an entire book to it. Besides, people far more capable than me have already written those books. I've read them myself, some more than once. (There's a list of those titles that helped me through-out my journey at the back of this book.) I do believe books with that level of detail are very much needed and stop you from feeling as though you are going mad, particularly during the two-week wait after treatment before you test, but this isn't a story of infertility. It's one of resilience, yes, but mainly hope and I need to start getting to that part, so I will offer a brief synopsis of my treatment experience starting with being convinced I'd killed someone while driv-ing and a luminous pink hairbrush.

Just a few days before one of our egg collections,

I'd become transfixed by the vibrant colour of my pink hairbrush. The same one I'd been using for years, barely giving it a second thought beyond the annual clean. Only today, I couldn't help but notice it resting on top of the black granite worktop. I was utterly hypnotised, in a trance-like state, obsessing over the colour of this brush for an uncomfortable length of time before my husband tentatively moved it out of my sight. Disclosure: I've never tried recreational drugs, not even as a young whippersnapper, but upon asking reliable informants, this infatuation with my hairbrush bears a resemblance to enhanced feelings experienced at many a late-night venue.

During another cycle I came close to packing a bin liner with possessions in preparation for a prison cell egg collection after convincing myself I'd knocked someone over in a hit and run. Just to add a dash more insanity to this scenario, I hadn't driven past anyone *to* actually hit and I'm not the best at running. I'd driven round the corner not even a few yards beyond our house when I became crippled with the anxiety of believing this had just happened. I was convinced I'd felt something brush past the side of my car, rather than just accepting the fact I'm terrible at reversing around the tree at the end of the drive, the one that's remarkably always in the same place every morning. Instead, I opted to burst into a manic flood of tears declaring I could reverse no further and requesting that my husband inspect all sides of the car, including the one furthest from the tree, specifically looking for any blood or body parts wedged between the wheels. He didn't dare question this request, probably worried I might shave his head in his sleep or something. Staying remarkably composed, he checked all aspects of the bodywork while tenderly reminding me I'd driven less than a quarter of a mile down the road and we hadn't actually passed another human being.

I honestly don't know if I can attribute this behaviour to being a direct side effect of the drugs. All I *do* know is that these induced hormone parties would bring about severe bouts of anxiety and a lovely little skin condition known as urticaria (AKA really bad hives), resulting in a year off work, the posh word being a 'sabbatical'. Another financial cost I factored into my quest to motherhood. Of course, there's no hard evidence to bring the drugs to trial, is there? It's the old chicken and the egg situation. What triggered it off first? The stress of it all or the medication? The medication or the stress? It's a difficult one to pin down as they both arrived as part of an all-inclusive package. I did tell my doctor about that breathtakingly pink hairbrush, and he said the meds could potentially be heightening my senses resulting in sharpened reactions, but then again, your senses are heightened when you're fighting, aren't they?

I felt a real lack of awareness and consequent understanding as a woman undergoing infertility treatment. I'd witnessed varying levels of recognition surrounding the bodily changes that occur during a pregnancy, the physical stress on the female form from pregnancy to birth. I'd read about morning sickness and post-natal depression. Thankfully, people have started *talking* about it because conversation provokes understanding, doesn't it? My own understanding now is that women are bloody remarkable and, although I can never fully relate to the physical impact and changes of carrying full term and giving birth, I'm still a proud member of the sisterhood and I think women are bloody spectacular. However, I'm not convinced society wholly *understands* the physical impact and changes that infertility treatment can cause to a woman's body and mind, and I've come to this conclusion because of the way it's bandied around as a simple solution, a cure even, much like a Lemsip. '*You can't have kids? Don't worry, just do IVF.*'

You should see the look of intrigue on people's faces when I tell them my boobs have never recovered. Granted, no one has looked quite as distraught at this loss as my husband. They gradually disappeared during treatment, without so much as a warning. Upped and left. The anxiety, unspoken depression, lost libido and self-esteem, you just don't hear about. The fear I had that I'd lost myself. Wondering if she would ever come back. You're interfering with hormones, your body's chemical messengers. I didn't always feel that the severity of that was understood.

Friends offered up interesting statements to soften the prospect of not having a child:

'*At least you'll still be able to fit into your jeans.*'
Or

'It's not necessarily a bad thing if you come out of this with your boobs not touching your knees.' (That's a thought, maybe they're just hiding down there.)

These comments are not helpful; they are evidence of a disregard for the physical and emotional toll a woman has suffered or is still suffering. She may not be able to offer up a visual aid to explain her changes. No baby as a reminder of why her body had to barter. There are too many women, more than we care to talk about, wearing their scars every day with no reason to be seen, no proof, just a memory of a time they tried. Really, bloody, hard.

Significant others weren't aware that egg retrieval involved sedation. As you can imagine, sedation of any kind for a serial planner like me was a source of absolute dread. For me, the sedation part was the worst ask. How on earth was I supposed to oversee what the hell it was they were all up to down there if they knocked me out? My anxiety was so horrendous during our first egg collection that the kind doctor only told me afterwards they had to give me enough to sedate an African elephant. They couldn't take the risk of my anxiety levels just burning through it. Me, sitting bolt upright midway through the procedure, demanding they handle my eggs with the utmost respect.

Sixteen.

They retrieved a total of sixteen eggs from that first cycle.

Sixteen potential chances.

Sixteen children, even.

Crikey, might need to look at selling up and just moving into a giant shoe like Old Mother Hubbard.

That was the wistful mindset when we first climbed aboard the treatment train. Even when we were aware of the stats, it's like when you're driving somewhere for a good old-fashioned summer staycation. You know there's a strong chance you're going to spend a week sitting in a mouldy caravan in the rain, but you've made the decision to go now, so you pack up your Uno cards and spend the entire journey reminiscing about all the trips of a lifetime you've never had in said van. The other thing was we didn't *really* understand it, not really. So, we did find ourselves getting excited over anything. The doctor could have come in and said my eggs were purple with giant green spots on and I would have probably only tried to take the positive.

In the beginning it was all new, a change from the sex schedule and the big P arriving bang on Q every month. It did feel as though something was actually happening. It's exciting when the eggs are retrieved, when the sperm and eggs finally get to hang out; we were only too keen to fill out forms and get our blood tested. I even got a thrill out of my first internal scan, especially after the nurse started practically salivating over the lining of my womb having three stripes. That's exactly the kind of internal markings a perfectionist such as myself enjoys hearing about. Apparently, that's a great attribute to have when trying to conceive. She did also go on to tell me my uterus was back to front; admittedly I was a little less ecstatic about that.

The novelty of it all soon wore off, though. Silent journeys back from the clinic, the looming realisation of those eggs needing to fertilise. The success story is not based on how many eggs you have *collected*; there's no egg collection conventions to attend afterwards, a chance to wave your dice breaker card about. (You'll only get that if you're familiar with Pokémon.) The reality is that it doesn't matter if one hundred eggs are collected, it needs to be *the* egg, and that egg needs to meet with a platinum piece of sperm, so it was during these post egg collection phases I started to become more acquainted with the lingering pain of treatment. My goodness does it linger.

We left those sixteen eggs in the safety of the lab, where later that day they would be introduced to my husband's sperm. We restlessly made our way home and waited to see if those little gametes had the same chemistry that two souls shared on a sticky, vodka-covered dancefloor all those years ago. We went home and waited for potentially five long blastocyst-forming days, receiving a phone call on each morning of those days informing us if the embryos were still dividing and separating or had experienced a cell death. That's basically exactly what it says on the tin.

Three.

We were left with three blastocysts from this cycle. And thirteen cell deaths.

(Thank goodness I didn't put the deposit down on that extra-large shoe.)

It was painful, even at that stage, before anything made its way back inside me; before any viable hope was given. It hurt even then. I couldn't cope with the lottery of it all, the misunderstood highs and the grief-filled lows. I didn't like the extra-long pause button my life had been put on, but above all of this, I still hate the way infertility treatment had the power to try to rob me of something I'd always tried to have.

Hope.

So, I'll be damned if I dedicate more than this short word count to it.

Casa del Música

I feel the gravel of a driveway underneath my trainers. I try to delay walking to the front door by digging my feet into the chunky, softly coloured stones. Twisting and pushing, alternating between my toes and heels. Comparing the varying intensities of crunch, the ultimate delay tactic. Sitting in the car for just under an hour, I hear the mechanics of the boot open. I watch a man sporting another one of his debatably 'cool' patterned ties lift out mine and my sister's bags before trying to assertively usher me towards the front door. He's needing to be assertive through fear of another six-hour stand-off like the one in my dad's kitchen that resulted in me smashing a pot of tea just a few nights before.

To the left of the front door, I can see a garden. Looks like they've had Alan Titchmarsh and co. in for one of those TV garden makeovers; it's full of flowers and shrubs, planted in all different heights and colours – landscaped, I think they call it. You can see a fair bit of work has gone into it. Beyond the garden lie fields, miles and miles of green fields with sheep sporadically scattered around. It's quiet, really quiet, which is probably why I was able to tune into the crunching of my feet. No cars or pavements with people bustling about, just a couple of sheep munching on some grass, two teenage girls and a bloke with another dodgy tie.

The oval glass panel of the front door I'm avoiding moves. It's opened by a smiling lady in patterned harem-style trousers; it's a nice, kind smile but there's no denying she's nervous too. Maybe he told her about my teapot anarchy. She's probably spent the last twenty-four hours barricading all her Royal Doulton in the loft for fear of the angry teen making her way down the motorway needing to move in for the next however many months.

The first thing I notice about the house is the smell. It doesn't smell bad or anything, quite a nice gaff actually, and I clock the carpet on the stairs right away, so it feels like an immediate upgrade in that respect. It's the *scent* of the house, the unique scent of someone's home. It's so overpowering, probably because that fight or flight mode we've all got mechanically embedded in us is well and truly switched on. This smell immediately makes me feel uncomfortable and I'm not all that sure I would have even noticed it had I just been popping in for a coffee, but I'm in survival mode. My brain is only too aware; it knows I'm not just here for a quick dunk of a digestive. I'm stressed and the pungency of this scent is only fuelling that. Although I wouldn't rave about the previous dwellings I'd recently had to leave behind, it suddenly strikes me how you don't usually smell yourself when you come home. When most young people open the front door to hang their coats and school bags up at the end of a long day pratting around with the Bunsen burner they're not immediately floored by another family's scent.

I did have somewhere else to hang my coat. Granted, things weren't going all that well back there and I wasn't rushing to leave a five-star review on TripAdvisor of my current home life situation, but it was *my* home. With the kitchen I could see my father sitting in, alone, on a single wooden chair, on top of a half-linoed floor, helplessly staring out of the window taking another sip from the bottle he was hiding in. Only nothing harbours without a price. For every sip he took, the drink stole two more sips from him.

Stank of shit, that house. Shit and emotional decay. I have no idea what went on in there before we moved in; I think there were a lot of dogs (I hope there were a lot of dogs), but I always remember thinking: *Couldn't she have made the decision to walk out and leave us in the other house, one with a bit of carpet and the preferred scent of Dettol?*

He would be sitting in that shit-smelling, empty house drinking on his own now we'd left; that made me feel really pained and very sad.

Above the label of '*Alcoholic*' by the way reads:
'*My Beautiful Dad*'
It tried to become the headline in our relationship, but I wouldn't always allow it. I'd grown to know

and love my dad since my mother had left. I'd seen snippets of his personality when he wasn't trying to pacify his wife's moods or his drinking. He was kind, I always felt he was kind, soft, intelligent, fragile, patient, but I'd never been given the chance to really get to know him as a father. I'd been busy being forced to pledge my alliance to the parent I loved the most and it couldn't be him.

I remember the first time we hugged. Really hugged. It wasn't long after she'd left, maybe only a few weeks. I was sitting towards the top of the latest set of stairs she'd moved us all to (on this occasion they came without carpet), convinced the previous neighbours had been talking about her. (Council house exchanges were a regular thing for us. There need be no long-term plan to warrant another one and there was certainly no logic to them.) He was towards the bottom, and somewhere between a conversation about needing to get to know one another better and how much he loved me, we met in the middle and hugged, for quite a long time.

This man became a person I would develop an unwavering bond with and a deep level of respect for and devotion to for the rest of my life. It takes a super-ior level of selflessness for a parent to admit they can't cope, to recognise and admit they need help, and he had, with his head held so very low, accepted that he simply could not cope.

I'm not saying it didn't hurt, or that I wasn't angry (remember the teapot?). Of course, at fourteen years old, I couldn't for the life of me understand why it felt as if he would choose alcohol over me, but what I came to learn is this:

We are all just teapots in human form.

Fragile.

Any one of us could be a stone's throw away from a breakdown or the ability to develop a dependency on a substance. None of us are above it, no matter what our residential or academic status.

'Do you like gammon?'

'What?'

'Gammon, it's like bacon with pineapple, do you like it?'

It's the lady with the genuine smile again; she's the music teacher from school. I know of her although she hasn't personally taught me. In hindsight I had my sister to thank for the lady's remarkable act of courage and kindness in stepping forward during a staff meeting after hearing we were to be moving schools, mid-exam preparations, because our proposed foster placements were not local. The foster carer directory was hardly queuing up round the block to take in two teenage girls. Yes, reader, these are exactly the kind of childcare plans made for vulnerable children who need stability by the truckload, which the government system are signing off on. She had listened to that proposition and, whatever her reasoning, she decided that wasn't OK. A virtual stranger must have gone home that evening and thought about it; I'm sure it must have been over a few evenings because that's a humongous, life-altering commitment. It's news most people would shake their heads at, offer a sigh, a mutter at best about '*how awful*' it all was, before reaching for another sip of their coffee and not giving it another thought.

Only *she* did give it some thought, clearly a lot of thought, and after she'd contemplated it, she stepped up to the big ol' plate with not a clue what difficulties could be on there waiting for her, but she bloody well did it. All I can think is that my sister must have been pulling out all the stops to impress her during those trumpet lessons. She's got massive, beautiful eyes, my sister – reckon she worked the old Puss in Boots sad eye routine on her while puffing her way through 'The Pink Panther'. Maybe the music teacher just liked us; we weren't exactly rebellious kids, too terrified to show even a whiff of revolt in case it made it back to my mother. Can't imagine we had *that* bad a rep in school. I only played a very small part in locking the science teacher in the cupboard. Other than that, we were squeaky clean and unhealthily polite. It wasn't uncommon for there to be a chorus of thank-yous or sorrys for the simplest of acts, particularly from my sister. I'd watched her flinch around adults on numerous occasions, which always made me feel a pang of deep sadness. This had been noted and raised by a previous school, but I had previously seen my mother be so charismatic, so wonderfully beautiful, articulate and together when she had to be, that once she flashed them that Colgate smile I imagine there were understandably no further questions needed.

We weren't getting smashed on blue WKD, smoking

weed, snogging boys or girls behind bins of a week-end, partaking in all the average teenage stuff, because we were too scared.

I'm not even able to describe us as 'good kids'.

Just . . . suppressed kids.

'Do you think you might like to try it?'

'I like bacon and I eat apples so, I guess so.'

It was around this time in my life I noticed the power of humour. I knew this was going to be tough, that the whole school would be talking about our musical sleepover by the end of tomorrow's double science. I figured out very quickly that if you get in there and crack the first joke, you're not allowing anyone to laugh at you.

It's not *always* the answer but I'd gained a lifelong skill in finding the funny when I could. I pulled upon it during infertility and who knows when I will be pulling on it again. Send in the clowns, that's what I say. That's exactly who I felt they'd sent me in with today, with this social worker of ours and his collection of questionable ties. Him asking if I'm *'happy'* with everything before he tries to leave.

Absolutely pukka, mate, and *when*, may I ask, do you think you will be popping by?

He explains how he will be back in a few days for a settling-in assessment and makes a crockery-smash-free getaway. Leaving us both to eat tinned fruit on top of meat with a woman I'd seen around the school a few times.

That, dear readers, is a reality of foster care, my reality anyway.

The startling truth after all the meetings, paperwork and decisions have been made. The point at which social workers help you over the state threshold with your bags then leave you behind.

When front doors close and children are left in houses, with strangers.

That's the cold, harsh reality of it, one I fear society likes to push to the very back of their '*this isn't really going on out there*' cupboards. A cupboard that most definitely needs to be flung open. Another misconception hanging around surrounding the care system is how 'lucky' children are to have had 'nice' foster carers when the truth of the matter is, there's not an ounce of luck to be seen when a child has no choice in entering the care system. You can try to dress it up any way you want, but there really is nothing 'lucky' about it. I've been on the receiving end of that statement many a time and while now, as an adult, I have an abundance of gratitude to this woman, ask me if I feel 'lucky' and my answer won't be quite so gracious.

I was still a kid when my mother had to walk out of my life, my dad losing himself in a bottle, unable to find a way out, my headteacher weighing me in her office because I'd developed anorexia in a desperate plea to try to regain some control amid the chaos spiralling around me. Still a kid when my sister and I found ourselves standing on the door of a music teacher's house, bags packed for the foreseeable. Me wondering if the boyfriend I didn't have was ever going to want to kiss me now.

Before an interim care order was granted by a judge in a faraway land there was talk of what might happen to us both. An unsettling conversation I don't believe I should have ever overheard between two working professionals. A deliberation about what splitting me and my sister up would look like. A couple in a seaside town would be able to take her but I was heading for the residential care home.

I've married someone who truly understands my obsessive need to know what lies ahead.

I remember watching *Tracy Beaker* on TV, and kudos to Jacqueline Wilson, by the way, who said she wrote her books because 'she found children's fiction out of touch with reality', presenting 'a world where parents didn't argue'.[6] She was slap-bang on the money *in that respect* and no doubt her ambition to challenge this narrative would have offered comfort to many children, me included. I'd always noticed when watching the CBBC's adaptation, those heavy fire doors in the children's home Tracy referred to as 'The Dumping Ground', the fire extinguishers stuck to walls, and thinking how it didn't look very homely at all.

I didn't really fancy the dumping ground.

Before Casa del Música there were others who showed a temporary kindness too. Friends' mothers aware of the situation who would let me stay. One who gave me my own room for a few weeks although I kept trying to creep into my friend's bedroom and she would tell me I really had to sleep on my own.

I definitely got on my friends' nerves.

I never really slept that much.

I was also too embarrassed to let her mum do my washing and was building quite a collection of dirty pants in a carrier bag under my bed. One evening I crawled under the bed, opened the bag and found every pair washed and neatly folded back inside.

Thank you.

Thank you for doing that.

I love my sister. Deeply. I don't know how I would have survived without her. The little armadillo always anxiously scurrying around with the softest heart inside. *I love you* and all your nine bands, and I should have been kinder.

In turn I have a deep respect for the woman who listened to the childcare plan presented to her while at work, decided it wasn't good enough and consequently put herself through that process.

I messaged her to ask by the way, only very recently, why she did it.

She replied within minutes.

I did it out of love and because it was the right thing to do.

I thought it would have been awful if you'd had to leave school.

She tells me of a little list she'd written on a piece of paper.

All the reasons for and reservations in not doing it.

Eight out of ten reasons for.

The only two reservations being:

Never having had children
and f e a r.

It's worth knowing that at the time of writing this book there are ninety-five children entering the care system in the UK every day. For the record, I don't think many of them are feeling all that 'lucky'.

Pink Elephants Don't Cry Over Split Tea

Pregnancy test day mornings came in a pretty consistent form, after spending the night staring at the ceiling. I made a pact with myself never to test before 6 a.m. My trembling hands received quite a sprinkling of urine while trying to get it either in a pot or just straight on the stick. The first test I did my husband was with me but I couldn't face the embarrassment of telling him it hadn't worked a second time or seeing the pain in his beautiful hazel eyes. So, for the next one, I peed solo. Later that morning, after I'd curled up on the tiny wooden floor of the downstairs toilet biting into the urine-scented skin of my hand desperate to avoid him hearing me cry, I just sort of casually, aggressively threw it out over our porridge how it hadn't worked.

One February morning at 6 o'clock, things played out differently. It was still freezing as most British mornings are. I quickly dipped my feet into the pale grey sheepskin slippers I'd placed to the side of our bed the night before in anticipation of the 5.55 a.m. trip across the landing. Of course, I could have avoided the past two hours of ceiling torment by testing at 4 a.m., it wouldn't have made a blind bit of difference, but the truth is, I didn't actually want the answer for another 120 minutes. I was sick of living with the empty reality of childlessness. I didn't want to go downstairs later that morning reaching for a coffee cup in my highly organised cupboard wondering how many more years I would have to wait for it to be filled with vibrant colourful plastic and missing lids. The novelty of test days had well and truly worn off, so I wasn't shaking today. Guess you could attribute that to the nervous system becoming well acquainted with the monotony of disappointment. I'd also had the genius revelation of it being much easier to pee in a large cup and just dunking the test in there. I bestow upon you all the vision of me sliding nothing short of a small saucepan under my nether regions, while sitting on the freezing cold seat of a porcelain loo. Two goosepimple-covered legs dangling over the sides, decoratively topped off with the grey sheepskin slippers (courtesy of the Aldi middle aisle).

I pop the pan on the side of the bathroom sink, tentatively remove the test from its wrapper and dunk the tip into my first urinate of the day, counting in pink elephants for exactly ten seconds, *but* as I'm in no rush to inform myself of today's fate I whisper:

'*Eleven pink elephants.*'

I place the cap back on (hygiene first) and rest the stick back onto the marble. (That is literally the only bit of marble we have in the house, I had to drop it in somehow.)

And wait.

I take my place back on the throne with the seat cover down this time and, while knocking my designer footwear together, count all the way to *sixty* pink elephants.

Two pink lines.

There are two pink lines.

I frantically scramble around for another test. We've already racked up thousands of pounds' worth of debt, so at this point I hardly think peeing on a few more tests would be considered excessive. There's nothing tentative about the opening of the next one, as I rip it from its wrapper before desperately trying to squeeze out another drip of wee. I even go so far as to abbreviate 'elephants' to 'phants'. There's a chance I might actually be pregnant here – I can't be wasting time on accurate zoological classifications.

Two definite pink lines, on both of them.

I lift my head in disbelief and am met with the silence of the bathroom, a reminder of my being here alone; he's not here. Why does he have to be so far away from me right now? Whose stupid idea was it to do this on my own today? Never have I wanted him closer to me than right now, I need him to see these definite pink lines, I need him to witness this next to me so he can tell me they're there. In this moment it feels as though he's sleeping halfway across the world. The journey along the landing back to our bed feels nothing less than unattainable. I fill my lungs with the deepest of breaths and, with one hand clutching onto both tests, try my best to steady the other just enough to turn the doorknob, allowing my release and a chance to make it across the landing, my metaphorical Everest. In truth, we'd already defied the odds nature had dealt us that morning. Upon reaching the top, I can't actually breathe. I'm surrounded by oxygen but feel as though there isn't any. I'm trembling as I lower myself onto the edge of our bed. A combination of nerves, excitement, self-doubt and sheer exhaustion from this morning's trek. I pass him both tests.

He slowly stirs from the warmth of the duvet he's snugly cocooned himself into, blinks a few times to clear the sleepy film from his eyes before taking a test in each hand, alternating his focus between them:

'Two lines, there's definitely two lines.'

Now, if there was a live stream camera in the room (and there isn't because we're not into that, but you do you), people would literally be yelling at the screen *'Throw your arms round each other! Profess your love. Start using sickly voices, at the very least offer up a tear, you pair of miserable gits.'*

Only we couldn't. Two pink lines resting on a plastic stick after all the heartache, pain, disappointment, and money burnt so far wouldn't lead us to believe we'd arrived at our destination. We weren't able to just start unpacking those suitcases of doom we'd been lugging around and start filling them up with new garments of positivity and parental possibilities. Trauma doesn't really work like that, does it? Your brain doesn't suddenly tell you to stand down from that constant state of anxiety you've been existing in.

You have to embark on a tiny bit of self-sabotage first, wouldn't feel natural otherwise. We sit in a state of utter shock, separate ends of the bed, staring at a test each. Holding them up to the light, turning them upside down, my husband's head and test hanging out of the bedroom window at one point, distrustful of the artificial lighting.

I turn to look at my husband who's repeatedly running his hands through his unbrushed hair. His eyes are most definitely awake now. He says he can't believe it; so do I. He asks whether we should tell anyone before both deciding not to. I proclaim how I'm only going to live off pomegranate seeds, more kale, water and chicken for the next nine months. I would now be needing to avoid stress at all costs and connect with every single one of my chakras before I leave for work each morning. It goes without saying my world championship weightlifting training (curling 5 kg on each bicep) would need to cease with immediate effect. He pulls me in for a hug and tells me he loves me mainly because he does but it's also his nicer way of telling me to stop talking. We allow ourselves a few moments of stunned reflection, smiling up at the same ceiling that had taunted me so many times before.

I had to go into work that day even though I felt I should have been granted the immediate authority to implement a national holiday. On the way in I popped into Tesco, as the very first thing on my new pregnancy regime was to give up caffeine. I scanned the aisle for something fruity, full of first trimester goodness. I thoroughly enjoyed reading the back of teabag boxes to see if my new dietary specification was listed. That was my first taste of it, those fruity teabags. My first taste of motherhood in a way, the need to care. I kept one of those teabags in my tea caddy for a very long time after the day I bought them. Sometimes, I'd take it out just to look at it. Then it split and I had to throw it away. I cried standing over the bin for longer than would ever be socially acceptable for a teabag burial. Many would think me odd, but I didn't. I understood the symbolism of that teabag, the hope it arrived with and why I found it so hard to let go of. Anyway, the proverb has always been not to cry over spilt milk, not a split teabag.

I was working alone in the office that day, just me, my new teabags, and the pictures of the positive pregnancy tests I had on my phone. I can now admit to doing absolutely sod all that day and happily taking the pay cheque. How could I possibly fill out Excel spreadsheets when I was pregnant? Not only that, but I had apps to download, ones that provided a week-by-week fruit and vegetable comparative for your forming foetus, and a phone call from the kind doctor to take. He wanted to know '*how we were?*'; a real sign of a seasoned fertility professional – doesn't ask for the result. Simply, how you *are*. That way, he gets the answer without having to face into the brutality of the real question.

He was genuinely very happy for us both. I suppose when you think about it, getting women pregnant (in the professional capacity) must be the pinnacles of these doctors' careers. They've helped create life, lives that would otherwise fail to exist. I mean if we all just stop and think about that for a second, that's an incredible skill to have on your CV. Makes the time I talked that customer into signing up for the company store card seem so insignificant now.

Then he just sort of signed off, super cool with a real vibe of *my work here is done*. It felt final. I thanked him, and he explained how the clinic would be in touch to arrange an early pregnancy scan. I told him I had a *Mamma Mia!* mug for him at home so would drop it in. During our time getting to know one another I'd learnt of his love for the musical. We would often discuss this during cervical examinations. Him, rummaging around. Me, humming 'Here we go again.'

Rather unusually for me, while pregnant I experienced a severe bout of optimism. I found myself unquestionably *trusting* everything would be OK. You may have noticed I'm not the sort to think Father Christmas doesn't have an agenda, so this fresh, new attitude was much like me having a lobotomy. I remember nights lying in bed with *me* reassuring my husband everything would be all right. Maybe it was the hormones, oxytocin reversing the effect of fight or flight, lowering your blood pressure, making you happier. On reflection, it was more an act of sorcery. Maybe it was the craving to finally reach motherhood, like when you're falling for someone all your friends can't stand. Deep down you know he's a bit of an arse, but you won't allow yourself to think about that because you want it to work out. I'll never know what I could attribute this unfamiliar thought pattern to, probably all of it, but I can tell you I'd certainly never been like it before. I'd spent most of my life convincing myself I was going to wake up dead, so having the capacity to reassure someone else *they* needn't worry was a new experience for me.

Another thing I found myself doing was obsessing over beneficial recipes for early pregnancy, driving to really weird organic food halls to get ripped off on some posh, probiotic yoghurt drinks. There I was, spending my days walking around with a fridge full of health-giving bacteria, an updating vegetable app, sore boobs and an extremely heightened sense of smell, feeling eerily relaxed about the whole thing.

I was getting a bit of a kick out of actually owning a secret, for once. Having had the whole world, his wife and every one of their cousins aware of our family planning affairs for the past however many years, we made the decision to stop updating significant others on the *whole* truth regarding our transfer dates. Everyone apart from my sister, only because she would have caught us out anyway. She's basically the cyborg from *Terminator*, a human emotion scanner who can work out exactly what's going on just by looking into the pupil of your eye.

The kind doctor had disappeared in a puff of success stat smoke and I was drinking far too much yoghurt. My husband left feeling like an anxious elephant, bopping, weaving and swaying his way around my synthetic positivity. While I was busy channelling my cockroach alter ego scuttling in for Happy Hour (they love beer, true fact, Google it) in protected happy hormone ignorance of what was about to happen.

Biscuit Tin Daydreams

If I'm to be totally honest, the greatest fear in all of this was not one of genetics, bloodline or even pregnancy. In truth, I was quite comfortable with letting a fair bit of the genetics on my side slide on past. I'd never felt that connected to the ancestors and I'd never really *yearned* to be pregnant or give birth. Not desperately. That's not to say I wasn't intrigued, or didn't want to be, but at the time I suppose I felt more aggrieved with my right to *choose* as a woman being taken away . It's something my body is biologically designed to and I'm only ever going to live this one life in this one body, so naturally it provoked a curiosity in me. However, during moments of great honesty with myself I felt I could, with time, *accept* not giving birth or being pregnant.

For me, the deep-rooted pain of not being able to have a child stemmed from the thought of never reaching the universal end result, irrespective of how it happened. It was the bit after the pregnancy and birth were over, after the night feeds and tiny nappies had gone, that I couldn't bear to lose. A trepidation greater than all of that was the one of never knowing, understanding or reaching motherhood. I just wanted to *be* a mum, to *love* a child. Love them as an adult, love them when they were laughing and love them even harder when they cried. I needed to love them even on the days they might not love me. I wanted to be silly together, dance round the kitchen, snuggle up under duvets consuming dangerous amounts of E-numbers. Cook blogger-worthy dinners and give them a Happy Meal when I couldn't be arsed. Walk little wet feet round the poolside with gap-toothed smiles and goggled eyes staring back at me. Share bubble baths with rubber ducks and pink smiling cheeks, crave a bath alone. To be asked why it rains and where the sun goes at night. Hold a tiny hand and feel it growing in my palm as the years go by. I wanted to give a look of disapproval while trying not to laugh. I wanted to be disappointed and really bloody proud.

I dreamt of out-of-tune recorder-playing and broken-into make-up bags, sports days, school plays and crying in an empty room on the day they would need to leave me behind.

I wanted to love and, for entirely selfish reasons, *be loved*.

By a person I'd had the privilege of guiding through life.

That's what I wanted, and it was the terror of not having *those* things that kept me awake at night.

This isn't everyone's only fear when faced with the prospect of not being able to conceive. The longing to experience pregnancy, birth, breastfeeding or the desire for a genetic continuation for some are also colossal parts of this infertility conundrum. I've spoken to and read of many incredible women whose experience this has been. The magnitude of that loss for many is, in truth, utterly tragic. I'm not wholly convinced the understanding surrounding that is quite good enough just yet.

Some might say I was spared another level of grief in that respect, and maybe I was. But the possibility of parting with motherhood, *that* was an adieu I was simply unable to make.

Lost in my regular reaching-motherhood day-dreams, thoughts of adoption had crept in. I knew there were children waiting in a care system needing, and so desperately deserving of, permanence and love. From personal experience I was aware there would also be children needing foster carers. I'd quietly toyed with this too but at this stage of my life I was in search of forever. A child I could wholeheart-edly love with no limitations or restrictions, who would stay in my life and me in theirs *forever*. I wasn't strong enough to love temporarily. If I ever did finally grasp motherhood, I knew I wouldn't be able to let go, and quite possibly all I knew of adop-tion at this stage was that it meant *forever*.

At that stage, it was just a daydream and I use that term truthfully because daydreams, in my opinion, are just not the same as serious, considered thoughts about a rather gruelling process resulting in the most important lifelong commitment you will ever make, involving human beings, most of whom are quite possibly already breathing at the time of your thoughts.

In my experience, people say they 'thought' about adoption *a lot* to adoptive parents. If you're about to become one, brace yourselves. Never mind 'winter is coming', you're going to want to get yourself layered up ahead of all those 'thoughts' that other people have experienced on your route to parenthood. The intriguing bit for me has always been how that sentence is not only the beginning but the end. I've not yet had anyone go on to explain why it never amounted to more than said thought. I suppose I'm also writing this as a tip-off before we bowl into these conversations, something to be a tad more socially aware of. It's rather baffling when your route to motherhood is met with such a discombobulated sentence. If you're insistent about sharing your contemplations, just see it through. That's all I ask. I wouldn't go up to someone, knowing they'd used a donor, and announce:

'*We thought about using a donor once.*'

Equally I wouldn't go up to a couple who conceived naturally and share how my husband and I thought about sex and having a baby once.

It's a bit weird, isn't it?

Enough of the righteous typing, back to the daydreams. Which were nearly always swiftly interrupted by reminders of a dysfunctional childhood. My palms would sweat at the sheer thought of a social worker learning about it, then drawing conclusions on my own parenting potential. I'd had a dabble with

Google one lunchtime and read something about the importance of a strong support network. The need to interview friends, family and ex-partners during the process. That alone was enough to make me think about flinging the laptop from the window for fear of them discovering my recent browser history, taking it as the green light to start probing around our lives. There was no way anyone would drop a child needing stability in abundance into our support network after the childhood circus I'd been rolling around with. Besides, the 'extended network' had experienced a drastic case of infertility social thinning of late.

Adoption felt like another route to parenthood that was too far out of reach. I wasn't 'perfect' enough and neither was my husband. We'd lived lives less ordinary and certainly weren't the couple out pruning the roses round our white picket fence after mass on a Sunday. There really didn't seem much point in tormenting ourselves with the potential roll of a different dice. So, at this stage, I didn't research the process any more than this. Although, another thought did keep creeping its way across my mind – one of a biscuit tin.

My headteacher wrapped her index finger and thumb around my wrist while I sat in her office one afternoon. I had started to get the invite quite a lot of late and I noticed these social events had now been upgraded to include a plate of nibbles eagerly positioned on the desk in front of me. As she releases her finger and thumb from my wrist, she asks if I'm eating. Headteachers these days, so *needy*. She's literally put on a spread of a few Mini Cheddars and a couple of soft custard creams and now she's expecting a Michelin star. She explains how she's concerned about my weight and asks if I'm finding eating difficult because of everything that's going on at home.

At this point, social services were involved. We'd had the man with the dodgy piano keys tie into the school a few times asking questions but I was still living at home, and although some days I wanted to stay there, my dad's disease had dug its ugly talons even deeper under his beautiful skin. His alcoholism reminded me of an eagle: they're extremely territorial and won't give up their prey without a good fight. Have you ever noticed the way an eagle will catch its victim, ruthlessly dragging it along tormenting it with the intermittent brushing of the floor, swinging it around in the air while they soar, sometimes dropping it or pretending to just so they can dig their blood-thirsty talons into it once more? To me that's how alcoholism felt: neglectful torment devoid of any care for its prey. There were mornings I knew he didn't want to drink but by the afternoon his eagle had proved victorious. The after-school visit from social services where my dad would dutifully be doing the ironing, without the iron being plugged in. A true talent, like the immaculate conception, only with laundry. So, in an ideal world in a different time zone, of course I didn't *want* to leave. However, I didn't like it there all that much lately either.

She was always on the ball, my headteacher; you couldn't walk past her with your skirt half an inch shorter than it should be, so there wasn't a cat's chance in hell she was going to miss a bit of anorexia on her horizon. I wasn't eating, I couldn't. Partly because I was in a state of perpetual anxiety leaving me feeling sick most of the time, and partly because it was simply a very obtainable way for me to assert some control amid the storm I was trying to hold an umbrella in. I told her, '*I'm not really a fan of Mini Cheddars or out-of-date custard creams, but I like chocolate digestives.*'

It wasn't long after this meeting I found myself a bit of a biscuit connoisseur. Every day after school, left on the edge of the bed of the stranger's house I was now sleeping in, I noticed a little tin. After what became a ritual of running my fingers along the image of Victorian ice-skaters with their fur-lined hoods and hands nestled in winter muffs, I'd push back the lid and nestled inside was always a packet of milk chocolate digestives. For every day while I was there that biscuit tin would always be full. I never asked my kind stranger to top it up and she never asked me if I needed it to be. It was just a given it would always be there and never empty.

A little tin left on the end of a bed. Just a little bit of metal with packets of chocolate biscuits. What she thought I was opening every time was a handful of needed calories. In truth, it was so much more. A tin of self-worth, a tin full of much-needed predictability, temporary stability and *care*. This stranger wasn't just *caring* for me because it was a part of her new job specification, she actually *cared* about me as an individual, and that makes for two very different things. She had no children, she hadn't fostered before, this wasn't a gesture she'd rolled out on previous occasions. That biscuit tin was a bespoke act of kindness carved out purely for me and I've never forgotten it.

It was the biscuit tin daydream driving persistent reflections on the importance of security, nurturing and care that children of any age need to thrive and survive. I had a mature realisation of the importance of stability and predictability, the potential of someone looking beyond my less than perfect story to give *us* a chance, these were things I would be *honoured* to provide.

Burnt Roses

This chapter references miscarriage.

I pull into the car park one morning, running late for a work meeting, but under no circumstances am I allowing myself to stress over it. In fact, I add another five minutes to the clock by rummaging around in my bag looking for a lipstick before applying it in the rear-view mirror. I'm preggers now, will be off on maternity leave soon, who gives a hoot about the work schedule?

I casually empty my business bag, a new routine I've been implementing for a few weeks now. I don't want to carry around anything that isn't necessary. Out comes the 5 kg make-up bag full of out-of-date mascaras and the book I have every intention of reading during the lunch breaks we don't really get.

As I've mentioned, during my time of pregnancy all my anxieties and worries just packed up and left. I'd spent 99.9 per cent of my waking hours prior to this functioning with a constant feeling of *what if?* What if my headache is a tumour? What if my husband falls out of love with me? What if climate change does exceed that 1.5 degrees Celsius? What the hell will become of us all then? I had a platinum membership to the fight or flight club; that mindset had become inherent and, let's be honest, the rollercoaster ride of infertility treatment doesn't exactly help anyone suffering with anxiety. It's like asking someone who can't swim to jump off the highest diving board into the deepest part of the pool, with no life jacket.

But those anxieties had gone. All of them. During a time in my life when you would have thought my brain would have gone above and beyond to try to self-sabotage even more than usual, it just stopped, sat there, silent. I wasn't worried. I didn't worry, not once, about not carrying this pregnancy to full term. I was too busy developing a very unhealthy addiction to the fruit app. I wanted to believe we'd won somehow. We'd scuttled out of the ruins, 'The Mighty Cockroach' sporting a slightly more flattened stature, unable to fly but still holding onto a set of wings. Infertility hadn't stolen our wings entirely and all we had to do now was what those around us had been doing – live. We just had to live, look after ourselves and one another, to eat, breathe, rest, love but no longer fight for something so easily obtainable to others.

Of course, I was aware of miscarriages. I knew they happened; I didn't need to question the prospect of one because it wasn't going to happen to me. What would have been the point of it all? The treatment, the money, the pain. Why would life allow us to see those two lines, why would whoever or whatever the hell it is looking down on us all allow that to happen? Why would the universe sit back and watch me finally taking my foot off the gas and relax? There was no need. We were seasoned to disappointment by now, we'd learnt to get comfortable with grief. As far as I was concerned, we'd done our time.

I waltz on into the meeting rolling my eyes at the boss about those darn traffic lights, bring out my box of teabags and set up camp for the morning. It's the usual sort of format, neither of us wanting to be there but cash doesn't come for free so here we are. She starts to do my 'review'. I display all the right 'review' behaviours, obligatory nod, intrigued frown followed by the classic '*Thank you for bringing that to my attention.*' It's your fairly standard working day. Only, I have a secret.

Today's review venue is a bit of a posh one, with those cup/mug things with the curled handle for you to try and grab a hold of. The curtains are floor length, with unnecessary balled tassels stitched along the seams. I'm sitting on a light grey sofa with a white damask print. I really don't want to drop my cup/mug. There's a round table between us, just enough space for two laptops and a pot of tea.

She starts to talk about my career progression options, which I have no interest in. She gets up a spreadsheet on the screen, starts flashing around the odd incentive then asks if I can even see what it is she's trying to impress me with. As it happens I can't, so in a bid for a head start on the £30 Pizza Express incentive voucher, I ask if she would like to sit next to me. As she begins to slide her things across the table in preparation to relocate, I start to feel a twinge in my right side. It isn't painful, more mildly uncomfortable. Enough to notice it's there, not enough to cause panic. I calmly readjust myself on the posh sofa in hope of finding a position the twinge would prefer. I'm pregnant, it's not unusual to feel uncomfortable when you're pregnant. A part of me actually enjoys feeling something because it makes it that bit more tangible, real. It makes me feel as though I really am pregnant and gives me even more reason to believe I'm on the home stretch to reaching motherhood.

She's talking about my team now. She wants a couple of corporate 'quick fire' performance updates on each member. Only the twinge hasn't subsided. It's aggressive, a piercing, twisting sensation in my side like the thick, curling metal of a corkscrew you forcibly twist and stab into a bottle of wine. It's not an act that takes all that long, removing a cork. Just a short period of committed force, until it's done.

Even I, in the desperate state of *'we've had our quota'* mindset that I'd cocooned myself in, knew this feeling wasn't a great sign, but it didn't happen again, not for the rest of the day, the next or even the one after that, so I pushed it right to the back of my negativity cupboard and continued to believe I was still on track to catch the 09.53 to motherhood.

We'd been invited to a baptism, a joyous occasion,

one I actually fancied attending, for once. I could go with no need to spend the journey there planning escape routes ahead of the '*Do you think you will ever have children?*' question time session. It was an afternoon kick-off, there was no need to rush; as it was still only morning I could start the beauty overhaul a little later. We decided to do what any responsible adult would choose to do with their free time, watch documentaries about people falling in love online with people they'd never met, before the authenticity of these online lovers is put to the test by a team of cameramen chasing them across America. Sadly, most of these romances result in what's known as a Catfish, but it does make fascinating viewing. I also need my husband to be aware of this show; if anything were to happen to me and Miss World starts messaging him, he must know it's a scam and remain forever in mourning for me. We snuggle up under a duvet in our musty dressing gowns. We don't wash our dressing gowns enough. The thought behind sharing that level of detail with you all is hope of a better future for our gowns.

Once I've found the premium position enabling me to reach both snacks and the remote, my bladder decides it needs to unload. It does this on purpose. I clamber over my husband; I could just walk around the coffee table but then he might fail to notice all my tutting efforts. Besides, *why* should he get to carry on watching and snacking in blissful comfort if I can't? I'm the pregnant one. I make it into the icebox that is our downstairs loo without dribbling even a little bit.

I hesitate before lowering myself on the toilet in anticipation of the porcelain's sub-zero temperature.

I look down.
   Not directly at my pants.
   Just at the floor.
   I freeze.
   There's blood.
   B L O O D.
   There's blood.
   My soul CRIES.
   I feel it,
   H U R T I N G.
   Sounds dramatic.
   It was dramatic.
   I shake.
   I start to shake.
   I wipe myself.
   Speckled red drops on white tissue.
   Speckled, trembling, drops.
   I pull my pants up.
   Step back into the lounge.
   Sweating.
   Beads of sweat.
   I take off my dressing gown.
   I look to my husband.
   Crying.
   Tears, slow, hot.
   Whimpering.
   Tiny noises.
   I can't remember what I said. I just remember

watching it. A spectator on a ringside seat, I had a VIP backstage pass, was as close as you could physically get without actually being present. I was later to discover this was one of my earliest symptoms of post-traumatic stress disorder.

It's over. I know it's over. He doesn't, he wants it confirmed not by me, but by medical professionals. He picks up his phone with one hand, tries to console me with the other. I can't feel him touch me, don't hear what he's saying. His mouth is moving, he's looking directly into my eyes.

He pulls away.

Pacing.

Up.

Down.

P A C I N G.

I shout.

He shouts.

We start shouting at each other. He's on the phone, one foot up on the bench of the dining table, brushing his hand through his hair. His dressing gown belt is making him angry. It keeps coming undone. It's pissing him off.

He tells me I need to do another pregnancy test; I give no reaction. He says it again, slower with conviction this time:

'*We need to do another test, a digital test, do you have one?*'

I can't remember speaking, honestly, I can't. I remember him explaining we needed to see if the weeks were decreasing. The clinic's nurse is still on the phone throughout this whole shitshow of a conversation; she can hear it all, but I'm sure it's nothing new. The frustration, panic, swearing. She knows there's a woman who's beginning to shut down and a husband desperate to keep her shutters up.

I don't want to look at another test, I want the one we have. The test I have in my bedside drawer with the two pink lines, the pink elephant test. If I look at another one now, it's going to take all of that away. I'm going to wee on another stick and it's going to strip me of hope. It's going to read: '*You stupid cow, you didn't honestly believe you were actually going to have a child, did you?*'

I've done it.

—

Don't look.

—

Pass it to him.
'*Just four weeks now.*'

I scream, piercing, grieving screams. I scream until my legs start to give way beneath me, allowing me to slide my limp body down the wall until I reach the coolness of the kitchen floor. He still has one hand on the phone, trying to stretch the other across to me. In a matter of words she tells him I need to stay at home, to make myself comfortable until it's over.

I ask him to ask her if it's OK for me to have a hot bath; I know it wasn't advised before.

She said that won't matter now.

I want it to matter.

I want it to fucking matter.

'*Pass me the phone.*'
She's kind, tries to tell me how sorry she is.
I hang up on her.
I wait.
We wait.
Pain.
I cry.
Sharp.
He's silent.
We wait.
I cry.
He waits.
I wait.
I hear.
Splat.
—
I look.
—
I scream.
He reaches for the toilet roll.
—
He pulls the flush.
Two mammals, lying side by side on a bathroom floor. Just two whimpering mammals forcibly pressing the warm flesh of their faces against cold, patterned tiles in a desperate bid to feel.

I'd never had an out of body experience until that day. Never screamed from a place of primal pain unable to hear the sound I was making. Never noticed having the ability to dig my nails into the skin of a hand but no longer feel it.

This is a miscarriage. That was our miscarriage. I've written it truthfully and because, quite disturbingly, there *still* aren't nearly enough conversations, honest accounts and openness surrounding a loss so often described as 'common': as the NHS report, 'one in eight women' experience miscarriage.[7]

On reflection, the most haunting part about all of it was the next day. The way I called the clinic as soon as my eyes opened, asking to speak to our doctor. Demanding to know when I could hop aboard the insanity train all over again. Had they said I could start after that morning's coffee, I would have done it because I was vulnerable. Now our miscarriage sits as one of their success stats, displayed like a stag's head on a clinic wall giving false hope to others.

It's not just the act of a miscarriage itself that causes the pain. That's the root of it, but miscarriage is a big tragic tree with many branches. There's the immediate act of a miscarriage, then there's the post-miscarriage aftermath: social, physical, physiological. Having to call friends and family to tell them you were pregnant but you're not any more. Having to accept *yourself* you were pregnant but you're not any more.

Then came the first period after miscarrying, the one I was totally unprepared for. It came out of nowhere and left its mark all over one of First Great Western's newly upholstered seats. No one ever thought to mention my dates would change and that it might be a good idea to, you know, carry a few menstrual accessories around with me to avoid the top-notch level of embarrassment on the male-dominated commute.

These are the 'short haul' repercussions that take place in immediate days and weeks afterwards. Then there's what I've just decided to call 'the long-haul miscarriage effect'. This can consist of, among other things: friends sneaking off to have babies in secret; acquaintances frantically running to the other side of the road with a shiny new pram ensuring the impromptu meeting doesn't happen. Even more spectacular than the above is that people take it upon themselves to make the decision as to what information they feel you're capable of digesting. Now this is very dodgy territory for anyone involved. Personally, I didn't want to see or hear of any new bundles of joy arriving. By the same token, I found it absolutely wounding every time we weren't informed.

£30 Pizza Express voucher to the first reader who can offer a solution to the dilemma. (That's right, I *still* went on to win that voucher.)

It's a mess, a complicated, painful, inconsolable mess.

That's also the sentence I would choose to describe myself during the days, weeks and months after our loss. I did decide to leave the house. I wanted some flowers; I needed flowers to acknowledge our grief. That's what we do, isn't it? When we go to a funeral, when it's time to say goodbye, we bring flowers. I wanted to show some respect to a life that was so desperately wanted but couldn't quite make it. I wanted to acknowledge the very early stages of a human life because, deep down, I knew society might not grant me the right to that.

I go into a florist. I must look quite a vision as the florist is actually backing away from me, seeking refuge behind the security of her work table. I tell her I'm looking for some flowers. She clearly doesn't want to insult me, instead opting for a polite reminder that I am standing in exactly the right place for such a request, while nervously sliding her scissors off the table and tucking them onto the 'keep away from crazed women' shelf underneath.

There's a window behind her. In the reflection I spot a blur of plump, orange roses. I turn away, ignoring whatever horticultural knowledge she is bestowing upon me, and walk towards the bucket full of long-stemmed, vibrant-coloured flowers. I brush my finger along the paper-thin, delicate tops of them all. Forwards then backwards before I focus on just one, running my finger around the crisp outside rim of petals over and over again, until my husband stops this fixation by placing his hand on my shoulder.

They looked burnt.

Every one of those roses looked B U R N T to me.

B U R N T

I feel my husband's arm gently move across my shoulder, pulling me in as I stare at the floor sprinkled with tears and petal cuttings. I hear him ask her for the flowers. I cling to the fabric of his soft jumper as he walks me away.

Next Stop, Please Drive

How do you know when to stop? I've been asked this question many times and my truthful answer is: no idea and, no, this book isn't refundable. I feel I ought to try to come out with something sensible like stop once it's affecting your mental and/or physical health or relationships, but that just wouldn't make any sense. In my experience, *all* these things become immediately impacted the day you're told you need treatment. The impact is full force, I don't believe you can ever be prepared enough for it. It's like checking the road three or four times before crossing and still getting hit by a truck. So, if we were all to stop and get off in order to preserve our mental health, I don't believe anyone would ever step on.

Besides, advice like that would only make me a hypocrite, wouldn't it? From someone who wasn't sure if she even wanted to start swimming in the great unknown to slowly releasing the air from her armbands and practically drowning in it all.

Would it have made more sense for us to have stopped sooner? Probably.

Did we? No.

And here's the thing: *had* we stopped earlier, certain future timings wouldn't have aligned. Unspeakably beautiful things that I believe were meant to come into my life wouldn't have. So, it's with this lived experience of reflection that the only sensible advice I'm able to offer is: You do you. Stop when you don't want to carry on any more, simple as that.

For a while I don't believe I could see properly. Not in the literal sense, infertility doesn't cause blindless. (Every cloud . . .) What I mean is that for a long time, I had lost sight of what it was I wanted from all of this in the first place. What the end goal actually was. I'd often ask myself if the older me, sitting in some sort of luxury home (here's hoping), staring out of the window on a hot summer's day reflecting on her life, would be able to toothlessly smile knowing she'd stayed true to herself. That she stayed in her own lane irrespective of obstructions placed in her way and travelled her desired destination to the very end. Because what I only ever *really* wanted was to become a mum, and somewhere in between wanting that and having to fight to get it, I believe for a while I was fumbling around in some sort of infertility treatment darkness. I needed to switch the lights back on with immediate effect, so I could start to recognise myself.

We arrive at the clinic one summer's afternoon nice and early, bringing only ourselves. On the previous trip we'd chaperoned a tank of gametes from our former clinic in a bid to see if it was the postal code they didn't like. I kid you not, we transported a massive tank of the stuff ourselves. Our old clinic wanted over £200 to move the jewels from one side of a bridge to the other. That's the game to be in, gang, gamete transporting. We didn't have any extra £200 so strapped R2-D2 on the back seat with a seatbelt and introduced the contents to the sweet sounds of Mumford & Sons.

We didn't think it was that strange, but a mate of ours was a bit taken aback after encountering us in a car park. Us in hysterics pointing to this second-generation robot, him politely laughing, unable to divert his gaze from the back seat. Seriously, folks, when your infertile friends refer to just how 'crazy' their journey is, they mean it. If you've ever been able to start a family after one night in a Travelodge, you saved yourself a good few experiences at the *Star Wars* bar.

Travelling light made a welcome change. I'm back modelling one of the grotesque white and navy checked gowns they insist on dressing you in for these occasions. All a bit cruel really – not only is the situation itself pretty dire, but you have to endure it all looking like shite too. As I peer down to my varnish-free toenails (the egg retrieval fashion request) I notice my shades-wearing husband playing with the lace of his shoe resting on his knee. Cheek of it, he's sat there with a pair of bloody Wayfarers on, channelling his (considerably taller) inner Tom Cruise or whatever the hell he's doing, while I'm lying here staring at my freezing cold pterodactyl feet wrapped in a scratchy dishcloth. Clearly got the memo for two very different fashion events this morning. He's really quiet, so am I. Neither of us are making a huge amount of effort to talk to the other. We're waiting on the blastocyst results, detailing exactly how many this roll of the dice got us. By 10 o'clock yesterday morning we'd been told there were nine. Come 10 this morning, however, we're fully expecting those doctors to come through those doors to tell us our chances have declined to at least half that number.

The medical pigeon carriers arrive through the light wood, tiny windowed, double doors. Both consultants appear to be exactly the same height (I wonder if it's a job specification) in matching scrubs, both looking incredibly uncomfortable with the news they are about to impart. One proceeds to scratch his pale blue shower cap, the other cuts to the chase with rehearsed pleasantries which are swiftly cut short by Cruise who's clearly come for the facts today.

'*How many have we got left?*'

Silence.

'*Two.*'

More silence.

'*You have two blastocysts left to transfer; they are of a very low grade.*'

They say don't shoot the messenger, don't they? By this point I had not an ounce of willingness or self-esteem left to even try to make sense of the stats laid before us. I let the weight of my head fall into the pillow behind me, hoping the sides would just miraculously wrap themselves around my face so I didn't have to see or hear anyone or thing. Mr Cruise wants to shoot; he's loaded up and ready to go asking why and how? He's even accusing the whole thing of being a farce, daylight robbery, which I'm in silent agreement with. He asks if there's any point putting them back in. Is there any call for the psychological cruelty of another two-week wait, putting me, us, through it? He's conducting this entire interview still from behind his shades. It dawns upon me from the desperate break in his voice just why he's wearing those sunglasses.

Maybe he knew, maybe he *just knew* this morning when he got dressed, today would be the end. I have no recollection of the moments between being told and walking along the corridor to have the last cluster of our combined cells nestled back inside my womb. I make the corridor longer, wider, windier, desperately trying to drag the whole thing out. My aspiration of motherhood, the hope of becoming a family. My body shivers from beneath the paper towel fabric of the clinic gown. I note how my knees seem considerably more knobbly than when I last cared to look at them. I'd lost a significant amount of weight during this process but hadn't really liked myself enough to notice. Arriving at the door of the procedure room, I clasp onto the doorframe with one hand, clutching my husband's hand with the other, and without an ounce of self-control I cry, *really cry*, my frail body hunched over as I make vague recognition of our doctor from within the darkened room. I'd never had a transfer in a dark room before today; up until this point they had always been tormentingly bright. This baby-making team were either on an energy-saving mission or seriously running out of ideas.

I'm coaxed further into the room by a nurse; there's some random guy I've never met sitting on the strategically placed stool at the stirrup end of the bed. I feel the heat of a hand placed upon my shoulder and recognise the kind voice of our doctor. '*Do you think we should leave this for today?*' Without allowing myself a moment to breathe I look back at him through defeated laughter and tears.

'*Would there be any point?*'

He doesn't try to argue or talk me out of it. He looks really rather upset, defeated himself possibly. He liked me, I always felt that he liked me, maybe because I engaged with his love of *Mamma Mia!* I sincerely believe he really wanted to see us become parents. I liked him. I felt he had integrity in an industry open to abuse. The pricing structure wasn't his fault, but we all knew there really was no need to keep two low-grade blastocysts on ice for another day.

Today felt like a funeral. The lowering of a cold body onto the bed of a darkened room can't help but bear resemblance to the lowering of a coffin, a departing of a soul. My eyes roll up towards what I guess is the ceiling. The warm breath of my husband whispering '*No more*' is a comforting distraction from the wetness of his tears rolling onto my fist. It is in this moment I believe there to be no more hope and say goodbye to my dreams.

That's what this master of invisibility did.

The 'silent pandemic' that cripples too many.
Crept in and tried to rob me of hope.
I don't really like you for that.
Only, you can't ever *really* take something 'that doesn't belong to you.

You're Not Me

Many years later I have the courage to tell the story of the girl who had a mother and the mother who had a girl.

The girl who *wanted* to love her mother and the mother I need to believe *wanted* to love the girl.

In my experience, mental illness or similar disturbance makes you selfish. I guess you have no choice but to be, when you're trying to survive every day. But it's painful, you know. It's painful loving parents who are not well. It hurts when you're a child and it still hurts when you write about it as a woman, many years later.

The day I went back to find her, searching for some reasoning, she gifted me my long-awaited words of nourishment from a mother.

With her porcelain eyes filled with tears and curiosity from a heavy heart she asks me *why* I hadn't any children.

My eyes fixed on her hallway carpet, I'm unable to respond. As I reach for the handle of her front door, she gently urges me to look at her, one final time.

'*Don't not become a mum because of me. You're not me.*'

I inhale as I type this.

Breathing in every letter of every word of this sentence she gave to me.

She knew nothing of my quest. I never mentioned it. She'd never hugged me or told me it would be OK any time a cycle failed, she'd never heard my thoughts or listened to my fears of never becoming a mother. Yet she wanted to check, she needed me to know, if I wanted to.

I was capable.

And I believe that to be her greatest gift to me.

Because I want to.

Itching for a Sabbatical

Dear readers, if you're still with me, I'm at great risk of this turning into a terrible handbook: *How to Live After Infertility*. People talk about a 'grieving period' but what does that even look like? How can we draw it? Write about it? Judge anyone for not doing it correctly if we don't even know what it looks like? If you Google it, you're told it means: *To resolve the emotional and life changes that come with death.* Stopping treatment didn't grant me a permit to grieve for a death. I needed Google to tell me how to grieve for something you never had. How to grieve for the loss of a biological child, because it is a loss, and I felt it important to really process, understand and accept that before I even contemplated taking another step in any other direction.

Only I had no idea how to do it, or *how* I would know when I'd finished doing it. How could I even be sure I'd done it properly? There's not a huge amount of advice out there for this, is there? The grief of what never came to be is barely represented in movies or soaps, there are no hit ballads to cry along to in the car, or sonnets to ponder over (if that's your thing). It's really quite a lonely heartache. There's no universal death bond in a sense because not everyone will experience it. All I knew was, I hoped it would pass, quickly. I wanted to wind the back of an antique clock and impatiently sit by it until formally notified that my grieving period was over.

By day, for around six months, my grief came across as a very pleasant, together woman with a high-powered job, and a good skincare and gym regime. I was able to both wash and dress myself, get to work, eat, pay my bills, and spend hours online shopping for materialistic clutter I simply did not need. By night, I could never sit in silence, watch a film, read a book or relax in a bath. I had to be busy, planning, or working, cleaning out cupboards, hoovering stairs or shopping online. By bedtime I could hear my heart vigorously beating through my ears, a reminder I was indeed still here. A stark contrast to my daily reality of not feeling as though I was. Dreams would consist of waking up having miscarried, holding a child's hand, crying, or starring in *Mamma Mia!* beside my doctor. I could never be in, behind or beside a moment. High-functioning anxiety, I believe it's called; PTSD is what I was later to be diagnosed with. I'm not attributing my entire diagnosis solely to our infertility – that wouldn't be true. I do believe it to be a trigger point to an adult child of a very dysfunctional childhood, and don't we all have triggers? Hasn't every human being somewhere down the line suffered? Are we not only one life event away from struggling mental health? I'm a cockroach, I pride myself on the ability to come scuttling out of the ruins, being able to swim underwater apparatus-free for forty minutes, you already know that, but even *we* can only scurry *headless* for so long.

On the surface I appeared OK, I was good at painting those surface pictures, could have had a lifetime of 'appearance' artwork exhibited. Eventually, though, it was my body that started to expose the truths behind my mental fragility. I would try to ignore the soles of my feet and tissue paper skin between my toes being tormentingly itchy when trying to sleep. I would wake up every day with a burning sensation crawling all over my body. My stomach, back, arms, head, fingers, neck, legs, feet and wrists had become covered with raised itchy rashes, and they wouldn't go away. It wouldn't stop. I'd been prescribed various antihistamines, advised to stop exercising, cut out caffeine and avoid emotional distress. I was able to action two of those. I was diagnosed with chronic urticaria, a rare case of severe hives where skin rashes persist, possibly for years. This I believe to be my body physically unable to accept any more psychological pain.

Our bodies are designed to protect us, healing our cuts and fighting disease by repelling things that are foreign. My body was repelling this pain, it was telling me to stop, for now. My skin was craving me to stroke it, my body needed to know I still loved it, *I* needed to *feel* loved. I hadn't failed. I just needed to rest. Bullfrogs can survive for months without deep sleep, in a state of minimal activity called estivation. They never quite reach an inattentive state, and can still respond to pain. If you touch their skin, you can cause it to burn, and I wanted so desperately to be touched and not burn. I wanted to sleep, I needed to close my eyes and sleep without burning, scratching or crying because it felt like absolute bloody torture. I had to reach an inattentive state, just for a while.

We were in no financial position for me to take any time off work, but there wasn't really a choice to be made. My husband was so concerned about my health and, not wanting me to feel guilty for not working, asked me to take time off, for him. It's the ones that love you the most who can see when you're about to break, and he wouldn't let me. He picked me up and protected me when I was full of fractures, but he never watched me break.

My employers referred to this time as a 'sabbatical'. A way for me to take a significant period of time away from the career I'd built without losing my job, in the hope that it would be the old me returning and not this hive-covered, highly-but-*not-really*-functioning woman they'd had representing them. I think most people take these when they're younger and want to travel round Asia, a chance to discover other cultures, returning with a more informed mindset. I was just going home to itch and sleep-train myself.

I factor some of this cost into the financial grand total lost throughout this journey, the financial debt we are *still* paying back. This and the £60-a-go therapy sessions throughout. No one mentions the cost of any of this when you're sitting next to the fish tank. The clinical representatives, knowing the lasting impact this can have, should have spelled out the finances needed to cover a long journey such as we, and many other people, have had. Not only the cost of treatment itself but the investment in therapy and the possible inability to continue earning if you simply cannot cope. There is no financial advisor sitting at the other end of the tank prepping you for possibly one of the biggest financial losses of your life.

I'm aware there are more schemes now, such as buy three cycles and get your money back (in part) if it doesn't work, and the first not-for-profit fertility clinic has now opened in the UK (praise the higher power), but I come from the days where people were spending more on this than others were on a house deposit, and some have even been known to have no house left to stand up in afterwards. To hear that one of the most lucrative markets in the medical sector may be starting to face proper ethical scrutiny makes me want to dust off my tap shoes. Here's hoping for a world where people are no longer sold add-ons without explaining properly what evidence, if any, they have behind them, and with more regulation surrounding surprise invoices for tests, drugs, storage and frozen transfers that were not included in the explanation when you signed the original cheque.

We used some inheritance from my husband's late father to whom I'm giving a massive book shout-out. My father-in-law was a truly wonderful, hardworking, self-made, honest man. Your son loved you very much and I thought you were rather lovely too. Sadly, I hear this a lot from people who've had treatment – it was only an inheritance that gave them the opportunity to try. Never has a relative's lifetime of hard work had the ability to bring such joy and guilt. When it's worked, I've heard people say it's what their relatives would have wanted them to do with the money. When it hasn't, you carry this weight of guilt that you wasted it somehow; that's how *we* felt anyway. Shame for the individual who worked all those hours. Day after day, week after week, month after month for years only for you to go and take one long trip down the infertility slot machine strip, lured in by the clinic's bright lights and free coffee. There's a thought – I might write *Infertility: The Musical* after this.

I spent my scratchy sabbatical scratching, reading, trying and failing miserably to meditate (I tried joining a class once and asked how long it took exactly to reach enlightenment; it's safe to say it's unlikely that I'm heading for Nirvana anytime soon), sleeping, gardening and thinking, then trying not to think *too much*. There were days I would cry, days we would laugh. Days he was silent, days he was animated, days we were numb and days we could feel. You couldn't ever really predict it. There wasn't a 'grief schedule'; it just played out how it wanted to and we were merely invited along.

There was a *cycle*, I suppose. I hate to sound clichéd but there was a definite *cycle of grief* playing out. The hardest lap to shake off was the anger, which wrapped itself around me like one of those fluorescent 1990s slap band bracelets. Anger for the unjustness of it all. The battle we had fought so hard in order to be given the right to do something so simplistically beautiful and supposedly natural.

Love a child.

I really wasn't a very nice person to be around during the wristband part. I couldn't see the glee in an awful lot of things or even attempt to dig deep enough any more to *try* to find some for others. I had nothing nice to say about those who got pregnant straight away, or those announcing their third. I was turning pretty sour. Bitter, some might say, but that can happen to anyone, even Mary Poppins. Don't try and tell me all that 'spoon full of sugar' nonsense wasn't her really saying '*swallow the medicine politely and try not to be a bitch*'. Wearing the wristband didn't make me a bad person; it made me a hanging on by my fingernails to prevent me slipping off the cliff edge personality type. It merely meant I had to focus all my energy on getting up and successfully putting my pants on for the day; there was simply nothing left of me for well wishes and pleasantries.

I can tell you what else this year consisted of: a ton of therapy. That's right, we were back on the sofa chatting to our very own Oprah and I could tell she had mixed emotions of being rather pleased to have us back on the show and sad that we were commissioning a second series.

We would cover off quite a few topics during this time. My mood swings, his mood swings, the *whys?*, *what ifs?* and recurrent *What the hell are we going to do nows?* I'd never seen our life together as childless, from the minute I got my head around the fact I didn't really want to shake him off. He just instinctively had it in him to be such a brilliant dad. He's incredibly affectionate; I mean the guy's literally walking around with buckets of love spilling over and he ended up with me, poor sod. The 'Affection Repeller'. Only he's so good at it, I did an awful job of fending him off, and if his persistence and patience could rub off on my cockroach exterior, then I felt it would be a tragedy beyond words for him not to have the opportunity of fatherhood. As the grieving period slowly ticked on, any time someone tried to sell us a life of kid-free mealtimes and exotic holidays, I felt utterly depressed. We *wanted* to spend the next decade picking up flicked peas from the floor and entering the campsite dance competition.

Something had changed within me since uniting with this remarkable being. The capability of falling *in* love and allowing myself to *be* loved. Learning how happy, stable homes and marriages breathe. Accepting the non-existence of perfection. Knowing sorry makes you vulnerable but not unlovable. Recognising maternal love isn't only what you're told. So, every night I would ask the universe:

Why?

Why have you taken me all the way here only to prevent me from loving further.

'*Have you thought about adoption?*' Oprah asks during a session from the comfort of her high-backed chair and crackling fire. If she'd had a cat to stroke, you could have mistaken her for a Bond villain.

'*You've shared throughout how this has always been about the desire to become a family. Have you thought about adoption being a way to create that?*'

I feel every hair sharply stand on the back of my neck and arms. In just one sentence not only has she proved she's actually listened, but our instinctual desire has been validated, recognised even, and she's made it all sound really quite simple just at that moment.

We talk about becoming a mother to a child I did not give birth to and how that may feel. I tell her in an instant how I don't believe that would change how I wanted to love. I share how I'd heard a quote once about children only ever being on loan to their parents, and thought it quite powerful. I explain how I'm not in search of ownership, just the opportunity of motherhood. We talk of children in need of stability and permanence. How as a couple we really felt we could walk alongside a child on an undoubtably complex path but that didn't unnerve us enough not to want to explore it. I wasn't frightened of complexity, I didn't need to be the only part of someone's story, I just wanted to be *in* one. I tell her about the little girl on the wall who used to stalk the Sunny D family. The one who had yet to learn that the strains of maternal love she would receive throughout her life would come in many forms, contrary to pretty much what it said in the contents of every bookshelf in all of the schools she'd attended. I speak about how I have no regrets about trying treatment but on reflection how bizarre it seems for someone who is quite comfortable with relinquishing genetic ties and not consumed by the need to give birth to have put myself through it time and time again.

Then I tell her about the clinic worker who asked if I would like to donate any of my ripe, under-35-years-of-age eggs to another woman. Throwing in the offer of a discount on another cycle if I were to agree, before a swift change of tune after flipping to the other side of his clipboard. Must have read 'Genetic history of suspected mental illness' in my notes, resulting in a quick retraction of his once in a lifetime offer. I go on some rant about how all of that rattled my cage a bit, expressing the embarrassment surrounding the rejection of my perceived damaged goods (which if I'm honest, I wouldn't have been selfless enough to donate anyway). Then retracting all of the above and expressing how maybe it's sensible.

The truth behind the rant is me confiding my insecurities about not being good enough, branded a black sheep, my capability of motherhood being judged on the basis of someone else's before I'd even been given a chance. How the hell was I supposed to prove to a load of social workers who'd understandably be leaving no stone unturned that I would make a suitable mother when my eggs had already been issued a one-way ticket to the bin?

The biggest fear I had when thinking about adoption was the process itself. The scrutiny I knew we'd be under, the cans of truth I would have to crack open. Scrutiny and cans you didn't have to crack open if you could just sneak off and have a biological child. That coupled with the fact my husband had hardly been the

Sugar Plum Fairy back in the day made me question whether there would be much point in wasting any of my unlimited minutes on a rejection phone call.

I tell Oprah what my mother said to me in the hallway.

How she told me that *I wasn't her*.

I tell her how I thought that a kind thing to say to me.

She smiles and tells me to hold onto that.

I smile at the floor and tell her I will.

She ends the session with her usual trademark: a casual parting statement full of untapped wisdom for you to analyse the cat's arse out of for the entirety of next week.

'*I wonder if your life experiences could make you the parents these social workers are looking for?*'

Then she evaporates into a cloud of aromatic smoke and closes her beautiful front door, leaving us standing on a tiled porch clutching the very last scents of aromatherapy oils and smoked firewood. Leaving us wishing away the week ahead so we could sit back on the sofa with Puff the Magic Dragon and her wisdom once more.

(Psst . . . when a therapist uses the word 'wonder' they're not actually wondering, it's a trick. They know the answer, they just want you to discover it.)

Whole Lotta Love

I recall a haze of Google searches involving the pros and cons of adopting through an agency versus a local authority and vice versa, a sudden increase in Amazon book orders, podcast listening and staring at walls imagining what it must feel like to meet your child for the very first time. Wondering how old they might be when you meet them, what they might look like before cautiously suppressing flutters of hope from within. We researched inter-country adoption (adopting from a country other than your own), which some people seemed to consider the initial starting point for adoption. I can write that statement from experience. We were asked countless times what country we would like to adopt from when we disclosed that we were looking into it. I can understand the assumption that the children more in need of a family are those from countries in the Global South that have endured conflict, political instability and poverty. But I have to admit that I was also unaware (probably because our government has a knack for brushing these numbers under the political carpet) of just how many children *here*, in our westernised, democratic country with a social security and healthcare system, are also very much in need of permanence. How many of these children not millions of miles away, possibly only metres from our very own doorsteps, are in need and so deeply deserving of love. Children who have been left to sit in an increasingly under demand, under-resourced care system, with no deadline as to when that wait may come to an end.

Every single child in every corner of the world deserves the right to a childhood – that goes without saying – but what it came down to, for me, was how comfortable I felt with the process. Cost was a factor, as the UK process involves only the cost of a medical appointment, while the inter-country process could run into thousands. I wasn't informed enough to know exactly what that money funded. In our minds the process was complex enough, and personally, I didn't like the added factor of any money being involved. Besides, I didn't have any left.

Someone told me once, years before we started our adoption journey, how they adopted from abroad because they didn't want their children to be able to contact their birth family (clearly in the days before social media). That statement made me shudder then and still does now. Adoption doesn't grant you ownership over another human being, whether from another country or your own. Parenthood in any form doesn't grant you ownership of another person. I don't think anyone should be looking to 'claim' a child. Yet we so often hear of this, don't we? Take divorce, for example:

how often will children turn into pawns overnight with threats of how regularly their parents can have access to them? I think we'd do well to change the narrative on this and start recognising that kids are just small Homo sapiens experiencing their own thoughts every waking second of every day. We're supposed to be older, taller and wiser, offering guidance, advice and truth. Children are a privilege to protect and walk beside, not to be confused with a commodity.

For us, it was learning of these UK figures that finalised our decision to at least *try*. Our child could be within that harrowing statistic waiting for us to find them. Didn't we owe it to them to put our big underpants on one final time, stop obsessing over all the reasons we may fail and let someone else be the judge of whether or not we were good enough?

We rang voluntary adoption agencies (VAAs) and our local authority (LA, i.e. the council), the main difference being that LAs have children in their care and VAAs, which are charities, do not. VAAs recruit and assess prospective adopters and create matches for children who are in the care of an LA. The VAA will then receive a non-profitable payment for their costs. You can be assessed and adopt through either one. We went to open evenings, sat through presentations, and built an impressive empire of flyers. We debated in bed, the car, over dinner and texts during our lunchbreaks, over which would be the preferred option for us to start the process with. The LA said they had immediate access to children waiting, which could therefore result in a shorter waiting time for a match, while the VAAs don't have such access, but can offer lifetime therapeutic support to you all as a family. The LA claimed to offer support too, but this would mean relying on council funding and wait times. I didn't like the idea of a prolonged wait for a match and was enticed by prospects of our potential child having access to support without solely relying on a government-run system. One that I already had reason enough to believe was pretty broken.

It took just one Sunday afternoon flashback to my teenage self in supported living accommodation, after leaving care – complete with various neighbours (a grown-arsed middle-aged man) – for us to make our decision. He had stepped over the highly secure, half a meter high chicken-wire fence and excitedly announced how he was going to burn me alive in my bed that night. He liked to make such threats, usually on a Sunday when my support worker was out of the office.

Care leaver accommodation was, up until very, very recently, unregulated. In 2023, the government announced that all supported accommodation providers for looked after sixteen- and seventeen-year-olds would be required to register with Ofsted and meet standards from October that year 'or they will be committing an offence'.[8] Let it be known: there had been no legal minimum standards for unregulated supported living to meet, allowing inconsistency and downright failings in standards. 'Accommodation' was also given grace to include barges, caravans and tents. I was clearly very fortunate to have been provided with a council flat, but the nutcracker next door wasn't a huge selling point. So, I really wasn't all that keen on remaining solely reliant on the state to step in and support us as a family ten years down the line.

I would like to give a thank you to my support worker at that time who was pretty damn efficient when on shift, for that and for the way you wrote about me. I accessed and read my file at the time of writing this book. Your consistent positive description of my character made me smile: 'Intelligent and having no doubt in my ability to form secure relationships later on in life.' You noted the bowl I kept topped up with fresh fruit on every visit and commented on how unusual this was for a young person on a care leavers allowance. Look at me now, having written just over 62,000 words, sleeping in a house full of love every night and still showcasing a fabulous fruit bowl.

Any adult of the care system could access their files at some point in their life and if contributing to them fits within your job description, you ought to know that you are writing the most important words ever put to paper. Forget great playwrights or philosophers, you're creating documents of truth offering answers and deeper understanding. So, pick up your pens with great honour, write about them only ever as human beings and spell their names correctly.

We nervously pick up the phone one weekday afternoon whispering to one another as it starts to ring about what not to say and my husband miming to put the phone on loudspeaker, so he can hear every word. I'd rehearsed a few times how I wanted to introduce ourselves and our enquiry, which might sound a little over the top but it's not every day you make a phone call requesting information on how to adopt a child.

'*Hello.*

'*We would like to adopt.*

'*A child.*

'*We would like some information on adopting a child. Please.*'

A good fifteen minutes of rehearsal wasted. We get off to a cracking start by looking like a couple of out-of-touch buffoons, and they probably thought about hanging up on us there and then. When I think about it, though, how else is there to really explain the purpose of your call without getting to the point? Sure, I could have chucked in the rehearsed pleasantries and résumé, but I still would have had to spit it out eventually. The call handler was lucky not to have to sit through the commitment to my rehearsal schedule when playing Dinah Glass (the lead) in the school's adaptation of *The Demon Headmaster*, proving I have been both committed and reliable from a very young age.

We were on the phone for a considerable time, but it didn't feel long. Just right, I suppose. We'd had a connection to the charity already as my late father-in-law had been a donor, and when we'd researched their organisational ethos and ambitions, we really *wanted* them to be a part of our story. It was what I would refer to as a 'top-line' phone call, nothing too heavy, she wasn't probing for anything other than our ages and why we wanted to adopt. There were a couple of things I wanted to get off my chest: being a care leaver, with a husband who's not so Sugar Plum. I thought it better to clear the air from the start, avoid wasting anyone's time. She explained how the next step would be for an initial assessment visit at home before we could submit a Registration of Interest. We politely accept them inviting themselves over, and as soon as we've hung up I start panicking about how filthy the back of our kitchen cupboards are.

The next couple of weeks consisted of a lot of bleach and a watchful eye on one another's swearing, while trying very hard not to think about the visit every second of the day and failing miserably. Reminding ourselves not to start imagining '*what if?*' or bringing home a little hand in ours. Not mentioning it to anyone then confiding in random café strangers our hopes to adopt. When self-doubt crept in, when I'd panic at the prospect of sharing with them the story of my life, I'd think of the lyrics to a song I'd often watched my mother sing to herself, cocooned in the safety of her duvet and headphones.

I couldn't not forgive her for being unwell. That wasn't her fault. But I suppose I can't forgive the things it made her do. Maybe one day I will be a better person. I hope life helps me to be that. I would like to be that.

I'd wipe away hot tears with my little hand after whatever it was that would have happened, watching her through the crack of her bedroom door clutching a Walkman in her temporary childlike state and rocking in rhythmic time to Led Zeppelin's 'Whole Lotta Love'. An odd memory for me to draw back to in these circumstances, I suppose. When it's dark sometimes we reach out for some light, perhaps that's what we do. After moments of childhood darkness Led Zeppelin, among many other rock bands I'd become familiar with growing up, acted as a reliable pacifier and a light for us both.

It was a 'Whole Lotta Love', after all, I knew my husband and I had to offer.

How exactly do they measure that potential?

When I thought of assessment social workers, it was as if they weren't human somehow. I didn't envisage them as aliens in the literal sense yet there was a definite disconnect with the fact that they're just people with lives, hobbies and families. Like when I think of the monarch. For years I couldn't even contemplate the fact that our late queen would have taken regular trips to the very same throne the rest of us sit on. It's the essence of power, isn't it? That's why we think monarchs don't pee and explains the fear that a lot of people have (myself included) of social workers coming into your life and assessing your parental suitability because they have the power to give you that or strip your hope away.

Only it's not a hereditary power these social workers have, it hasn't arrived through ancestral wealth. Quite the opposite; it's a profession that is underpaid, overworked and under-resourced, full of people who have dedicated years of their lives to studying in the hope of making a difference to some of the most vulnerable children in this country. Children who have already been through too much. With power comes great responsibility, and I can't think of a greater decision I would want to get right than this. So, I can honestly say we were open to answering whatever it was they had to ask because it is *their job* to get this right. From the moment we made that phone call, we'd decided to trust in the system and its outcome. All we could do was present ourselves honestly.

Cleaning standards aside. There was no other way around it. No strings to pull, social status to sway (not that we have one) or cash to tempt decisions (not that we had any of that either). It was to be based upon the raw, unedited, filter-free version of our lives, and do you know what? I was ready to give them just that and be *proud* of it.

A Planet Named Truth

'You answer it.'

'No, you ... I come across a bit "off" at first, everyone says it. You're smilier.'

He opens the door flashing his rather large gnashers, with me awkwardly forcing a smile behind him in the hallway. We're both in our slippers; it feels odd to be dressed this informally for a meeting so important. I tell myself it's OK because it's in our house and they would be more concerned about our irresponsible ways if we sat on the sofa with our shoes on – bringing germs in from outside could be dangerous to a child – before me expressing how there's absolutely no need for them to take theirs off in a bid to look super cool and unfazed about the housework.

On the doorstep stand two women, one wearing jeans, the other a floral skirt. Jeans looks quite young, about my age, the other a little older, more my husband's. *Maybe they've done that on purpose*, I wonder. Gives them the ability to really psychoanalyse us one on one. Try and connect with us individually over a 1990s and 2000s pop quiz. They're perfectly 'normal' looking, no extra eyes, heads or tails, both very friendly and have no issues at all in making themselves at home, which makes me feel slightly more at ease. We sit on one sofa, they on another, before I realise I haven't offered them a drink so reel off the selection of herbal teas we don't actually drink but the cupboards are now bursting with. Jeans opts for a glass of water out of sheer politeness – you feel you have to at least ask for that, don't you, when you get the vibe of a host *desperately* wanting to host. She probably had a bottle of water in her bag but could see I was practically foaming from the mouth to show them my cups. Floral takes me up on the offer of a camomile tea, leaving my husband to break the initial awkward pleasantries alone. Which, out of the two of us, he is much more suited to. Amid the sound of the kettle boiling, I can hear him wasting no time at all in asking them how far they had to travel and, the *universal awkward ice-breaker*, observations on the British weather.

I make my way back into the lounge, distributing drinks and clambering over my husband's outstretched legs to sit beside him. Any informalities for me are well and truly broken by Floral asking, with a camomile calm smile, probably the most important of all questions we are to be asked:

'*Why do you want to adopt?*'

I try to answer, so does he. I stop to let him have a go, he me. We nervously repeat this pattern a number of times before he tells them our truth.

'We _____'

I'm bursting with pride for him, so much pride. He's not usually one to succinctly get to the point but he's pulled it out of the bag. You have no idea how your partner is going to react in a situation like this; I've never seen him in this environment before so there's no familiar territory to draw upon. He's acing it, speaking with such clarity and passion. Up until this point I haven't had a chance to see just how much *he* wants this. Yes, we'd chatted in great length about this route to parenthood, thrashed out potential fears and practicalities; he's pragmatic, my husband, a logical thinker, always up for a chat of that description, but I haven't ever seen him speak like *this*. Raw, honest, considered, yes, but *passionate*. He really knows what this means, the potential privilege of becoming a child's father and the responsibility of supporting a child in understanding the complexity of this journey for the rest of their life. He has no issues in laying himself bare (not literally); he shares our previous private discussions around trusting the assessment to be in the best interests of the children waiting and how he's open to answering any questions we would face during the process. Admittedly there's a slight discomfort at the prospect of statements from ex-girlfriends (most would find that uncomfortable, let's be real) but he manages to pull through it, admitting he wouldn't necessarily be flavour of the month but how many exes are? To which they respond that it's specifically ex-partners with children or a history of residing together that they want to know about, which provided some relief.

They ask how much we understand of the process and the children placed for adoption. They are both extremely informed and experienced, that's very clear, and the more they talk the more apparent it becomes that we are potentially stepping foot onto an entirely new planet. Jeans explains how the average age of a child waiting to be adopted is between two and three years, with boys, sibling groups, children over five, children from an ethnic minority background or with complex additional needs usually having to wait longer.[9] I don't even try to hide my reaction to this injustice. In secret, I'd always dreamt of becoming a mother to a little boy; the reality of there being such disparities in waiting times tinges my eyes and heart with sadness.

She begins to talk about a fairly new process: 'Fostering for Adoption' or 'early permanence', a concept initiated to minimise the number of foster placements children may experience by allowing the potential adoptive parents or parent to foster them initially until the placement order has been granted. (Note: The Placement Order is granted at the end of the care proceedings.) At that stage you could then apply to formally adopt the child. The positives for this process are that it is less disruptive for the child and offers an opportunity to parent and bond with a child from a much younger age. Research has shown that multiple moves between carers for children is damaging even if those carers are providing good or excellent care, so giving children the opportunity to live with their potential adoptive parents sooner is of great benefit to the child.[10] The positives sound, well, positive. Undeniably, earlier permanence would be in the best interests of the child and an opportunity for both parent and child to be together as soon as is viably possible, but there's a catch coming, I can feel it in the air. Jeans shifts her position a little before carrying on: *'There's an element of risk involved with Fostering to Adopt. Until the placement order is granted, there is a chance the child could return to their birth family.'* The catch being the Judge who will decide at the end of care proceedings if the child should reside in long-term foster care, an adoption placement, a family member or return to a birth parent/s.

She explains how if this decision to return were to be made, it would be considered the best outcome for the child.

I liked hearing this. I needed to have it reaffirmed to me that the days of children being removed from birth families because of unmarried mothers fearing society's judgement or poverty preventing families staying together are no longer viable reasons (not that they ever were) to remove a child.[11] I *wanted* to hear how some families with the right support and guidance need not be separated. In my mind, adoption should only ever be the absolute last resort whatever the circumstances leading up to that decision. I've always thought that, but I wanted to hear it from those who truly understood how the system worked.

The selfish side of me sat there listening to this in utter panic at the prospect of bringing home a child and falling in love before having to let them go. The side that's already years deep in trying to become a mother and *doesn't want* to temporarily love. *She* wants to hold their hand as a child, try to as a teen, and cup her elderly fingers over their grown-up hands for as long as she's meant to be here. *That woman*, if she's to be completely honest, only has one small teaspoon of strength left to try to cross this finish line. Although she wishes she could be that selfless in loving momentarily, she couldn't take that risk.

Floral chips in to explain how the younger a child is, the less medical information or insight into any additional needs there will be. She's very firm in explaining how we would need to ask ourselves honestly if we could cope with any possible future uncertainties. For example, symptoms and a diagnosis of Foetal Alcohol Spectrum Disorder often don't occur until school age. Again, straight to the point, and a significant point made too.

We're informed how relinquished babies are an anomaly. Practically non-existent. Again, something I want to hear. They talk to us about special guardianship. The rise in birth family members, when possible, stepping in, preventing separation. But they're not here to tell us of all the reasons why children *aren't* adopted. They're sitting here today offering complete transparency about the realities behind children being unable to stay with their birth families.

We're told of neglect, abuse, substance misuse, domestic violence and inabilities to care for a child. Each reason resulting in an inability to care for a child being incomprehensibly tragic. Some of these reasons are surrounded with such knotted complexities that many could *never* and won't *ever* have to try and comprehend them.

They really don't hold back and there's no time to reflect upon the tragedy of all of the above because they swiftly move on to explain how, if you adopt a child with no additional needs or none of these backgrounds, your future child will still have experienced trauma. Loss is trauma, and separation from birth parents at any age is still a loss, so please don't even think about filling out your Registration of Interest unless you can get your heads around that, because these children have already been through enough. That was the gist of it from Florals and Jeans.

I sit in awe of their advocacy as individuals and their dedication to their profession, and I really bloody like this straight-talking, no sugar-coating-it approach. They're being nothing but straight down the line. A stark contrast to the fertility treatment open information evening.

All I can think as I listen to them is how much *I want to do this*. At times it feels as though they've come round to talk us out of it, but it's had the opposite effect. I'm sitting here like a fly perched on a sugary doughnut knowing I'm not going anywhere. I can do complex, I understand relationships aren't black and white, I don't even like black and white. I know of a maternal love I've craved since childhood that hurts not to be able to give it. I've felt loss and indescribable pain. So have these children. There would be common ground in grief. I won't ever know how it feels to be adopted. EVER. But I'm desperate to sit and listen in the hope of a better understanding. ALWAYS. What this conversation has done is trigger an immense level of respect.

I'd imagined Love.

But respect is the feeling that has struck me down.

How could you not feel this in abundance for a child having to trust another stranger? Arriving with a suitcase full of history, needing it not to be locked shut but deserving of someone willing to hold the weight of it. Keeping the locks ajar but never closed, ready to open them fully when *they tell you* it's time because this is *their* suitcase and you have the privilege of being its porter.

I want to become a mother, to parent a child, and that includes all that comes before them, all that *is* them and everything that has made them who they will become. That's what I want to do.

How do we sign up?

The Traffic Cone Head and the Helpful Woodlouse

After you submit your official Registration of Interest, you become an unpaid senior data entry specialist. Filling out forms at lightning speed is a skill you didn't even know you had. Rest assured, you're about to become an absolute expert in the field by the end of the process.

There's a form for everything, ones to sign ensuring the form prior was signed correctly, forms for the cat, dog, and your financial circumstances. They're not looking for Richard Branson (other rich people do exist) but this is to assert if you're in a strong enough financial position to offer stability to a child. You don't need to be a homeowner and can be in receipt of benefits. Credit cards or loans won't prevent you from adopting (if you've had infertility treatment, I imagine that's a bit of a given); they just want to know how you're *managing* that debt. Home risk assessment forms, fire escape plans and the absolute showstopper for an applicant like me (having moved home through the council enough times to qualify for the travelling circus as a child) – the chronological life history form. This *pièce de résistance* requires every address, place of education, significant life event, career move and partner to be listed on two sides of paper. Well, I got straight on the blower and told our social worker they'd better start sawing a few more trees down out the back, as these two sides of A4 weren't going to get me past primary school.

Our diaries became full of social worker visits, some involving us being spoken to together, others apart – those are the ones you worry about because you can't kick your partner under the table for swearing – and paperwork deadlines. There were medical checks, not because you're not permitted any health issues if you want to adopt, but more to ascertain if there's any-thing that might prevent a child's future security with you, like some awful disease, I guess. Which *obviously* led me to believe I was now dying and would need to cease the process in order to plan my funeral instead. I even asked the GP's receptionist if the fee for this examination could be returned if that turned out to be the case. Can't even die on the cheap these days. Then came the required DBS checks – clearly a very important part of the process but, I'm keen to add, not because you're never allowed to have made a mis-take or some plain daft decisions (I stole a sweet from Woolworths once, thought it best to come clean). My sensible point is people make mistakes. You may have made one twenty years ago when you were young and carefree. Are you *still* making them or making the same ones? That's what the process is interested in. It goes without saying that a previous history of violence towards children, partners, or holding up your local bank in a heist, would rightly prevent you from adopting.

There is a misconception that the adoption process seeks utter perfection. Couples or individuals with the squeakiest of images, backgrounds and extended family dynamics that could rival *The Sound of Music* for wholesomeness. It would sadden me greatly if that idea were to hold someone back from making an enquiry at the very least. Perfection doesn't exist; these children aren't asking for perfection. *They're* not actually asking for anything. Adoption is a non-consensual decision for a child, we'd all do well to remember that. What's being requested on their behalf is stability. Security, nurturing a lifelong commitment, openness, honesty, advocacy and love. You don't need to be perfect to give that, just willing to give it your damn best.

Your friends and family might think they're getting off lightly with the odd phone call. Fear not, it soon progresses into paperwork and a face-to-face visit after a de-brief from your good self on how not to mention that time you thought you were *hilarious* running into bars with a traffic cone on your head. Even your employers get sucked into the adoption process vortex with a reference request. Thankfully, it's to prove you are who you claim to be and less focused on your dedication to the role. There really is no stone left unturned and not one person in your immediate network unaware of what you're up to.

Then comes the most awkward rock of all, the one you would really rather leave peacefully resting on top of all those wriggling woodlice you'd moved on from. Readers, may I present to you *the ex-partner reference*. I personally hadn't had a relationship deemed mature enough to poke around in, but it's fair to say there's a bit of an age gap between me and Sugar Plum, which left him awkwardly smiling with the prospect of an ex being asked for an opinion of him. My unasked advice for this stage of the process: stay cool. Don't let the wriggling crustaceans get under your skin. I've heard many an interesting ex-partner tale from other adopters having gone through the process and I suppose life's reality is that some are happy to see their exes move on. Others can't quite accept the fact you're no longer hugging their photograph and crying into your pillow every night, seeing this as an opportunity to stir the proverbial pot. Social workers are more than aware of this, by the way – ours even said as much. They're not looking for tit for tat (bet they get plenty), tales of who cheated on who or which one of you unloaded the dishwasher the most. What they're really after are any *serious concerns* regarding the safety of a placement of a child.

Before I swiftly move off the topic of ex-woodlice, I have just one thing left to impart. The experience could leave you pleasantly surprised. I bumped into the woman who provided my husband's ex-partner reference in a shopping centre many years on. She lent me a pound (I'll explain later) and I offered her a huge thank you for honestly describing my husband as the potential father I knew he could be. I thought she was really nice, *there's* a turn-up for the book.

I would be lying if I wrote this book without acknowledging the uncomfortableness surrounding some of the process, but do you know what? Never at any stage did I feel we were asked or had anything requested of us that wasn't relevant to the objective – determining suitability for a child. Children are reliant on Social Workers' decisions. We all shout at the news, don't we? I have. Very quick to point the finger at whoever got it wrong when we hear of some horrific tragedy involving a child and social services. I took a lot of comfort in discovering just how scrupulous the process was. I refused to be a hypocrite, angry at the failings of the system one minute and hoping to avoid any personal awkwardness the next. Our social worker made a very strong case during one of our two-hour questioning sessions:

'*These children don't need the process failing them.*'

In between my new specialist admin role, I found myself spending considerable time sitting on very small chairs. With no young children in my family or any childcare experience under my belt, I had to go out and get some. Mine consisted of an afternoon a fortnight in my local preschool, squidged in between a load of toddlers animatedly explaining to me how they couldn't eat their snack because they were being chased by giant alien spiders before asking me if I had any bogies up my nose. Bogies seemed to be the 'on trend' snack of choice during this time. A successful childcare experience afternoon would consist of me walking out of there, nostrils held high with *all* my green goods still securely nestled away inside.

I really enjoyed sitting on tiny chairs, realising just how quirky and downright hilarious little people are. Admittedly, I wasn't quite prepared for their straight-talking approach. Jeez, there really is no mucking about, is there? Say it *exactly* how it is. The good, the bad and if you're looking a bit ugly. Get more kids in Downing Street, that's what I say. I liked this participation part of the process; it filled me with a sense of pro-activeness. The ability to be doing something, the occasional feeling of grabbing some reins (which I never felt were there to grab during treatment) made the thought of reaching motherhood almost tangible.

We became very well acquainted with our social worker, a professional friend I would call her. At one point I contemplated clearing out the spare room and just inviting her to bunk up in there until she'd finished dissecting our life stories before compiling it all together into what's officially named a PAR (Prospective Adopter's Report).

Throughout this journey, my husband and I were constantly learning new things about ourselves and each other, some pretty beautiful (others less so) as well as interesting things I'm not sure I ever would have discovered had we not embarked on this process. I would highly recommend the no holds barred approach as a couple if you're setting out on this process. The adoption assessment is a bizarre period. For a start it's called an 'assessment' which hardly screams kick back, relax, then we'll tell you if you're deemed suitable to adopt or child or not. It's an assessment of your suitability and compatibility to this route to parenthood. You're undeniably under considered surveillance. That's different to scrutiny, though, isn't it, which is how I remember imagining the process to feel. I'd prepared myself to be under critical scrutiny in its highest form. I would lie in bed thinking of answers in response to all the critiques they were going to throw my way. Only that wasn't to be the case. Something I noted almost immediately was just how much our social worker *wanted* this to work. How sincerely she *hoped* to see individuals come forward to adopt and how willing she was to help them be successful with that decision.

It had never occurred to me just how much people in the profession want nothing more than to find suitable adopters for the too many children waiting. I can't imagine they enjoy catching out prospective adopters; why would they? What a waste of time and resources only to have to decline applications any further.

Interestingly, personal questions asked were less focused on parts of life I had no control over, and rather on how I'd responded to adversity and life's challenges. Had I accessed any support? Taken time for self-reflection and personal development? The thought of trying to connect with my chakras under a waterfall waving a bit of sage around wasn't really my thing. I couldn't get enough of therapy sessions, however. If there was a therapy loyalty card, mine would regularly have been fully stamped. I'd had therapists I liked, ones I didn't and some I had no opinion of at all. There was the really patronising one social services sent into school once a week to ask why I wasn't eating and if I knew *what food even did for the body*. The funded sessions years later where she spent far too long checking her clock to see when she could officially stop offering empathy. Empathy's not free, you know, not on her watch. The therapist who successfully challenged *the why* behind my unhealthy levels of perfectionism and self-criticism. And of course my most recent encounters with our wonderful Oprah. Never had I imagined that one day being a regular therapy attendee might just play in my favour.

Therapy should carry no shame, ever. The adoption process was testament to that.

You don't have to take a gap year to self-reflect either. I know there are some really wonderful exotic settings for it but if the next best place for you is sitting on a bus (it often was for me) or while you're washing up, it still counts, even if you didn't post the moment on social media. The bus was always a trigger for me; seeing a young mum with a pushchair and a couple of kids would always make me think of mine. I'd be sat there wondering what she was like as a mother when I was little because I have very few memories of those early years. I'd watch these young women acing it, juggling it all. I'd try to imagine her zipping up my coat, protecting me from the rain, because I desperately wanted to throw a ring out to some happier times and pull them back in. I knew there would have been some, but mine had nearly all drowned. I still find that really sad. I'm sitting there on the bottom of a double decker trying to ignite fond memories of my early years before I'm flooded with thoughts on all the ways I *didn't* want to parent. Behaviours I knew were wrong, I don't need to spell them out in a book. I just want to share how self-reflection is yours, you own it. There is no hard and fast rule on how it comes or what it will look like. The assessment process just wanted to know if I'd had a bit, be it on the top of a mountain or the back of a bus.

Just when you think you've conquered all the forms, you receive a load more. You're far from done. After filling forms comes compiling lists and logs detailing all your 'adoption homework'. Books, podcasts, films, documentaries, blogs, organisations, anything at all that can prove you now have a wider understanding of adoption than when you made that initial phone call. We enjoyed listening to the few podcasts there were offering an insight into adoption. It was a struggle to find many books we connected with, though, particularly my husband. He had the extremely difficult decision of choosing between the *two* recommended books offering a male perspective.

Then came the night-time forum scrolling, something I vowed never to do again after treatment, but old habits die hard. Pages full of horror stories and tales of utter despair. I'd noted this to be a running theme when it came to forums. I remember often gasping at my phone during the two-week waits after a transfer, usually while on the loo, reading stories of blastocysts being swapped in the lab and placed back inside the wrong womb. Or having a negative pregnancy test followed by a shock birth in Asda months later. *Proof* that the medical profession is not to be trusted, and instead we should all be following this guy who recommends we stand on one leg rubbing a rare bead offering a one-off subscription fee of just £200. Then came the fostering and adoption threads on addiction, mental illness and broken relationships. I found it interesting the number of people expressing how these concerns are what would prevent them from considering fostering or adoption. As if mental health, estrangement and dysfunction are non-existent within biological relationships.

No one will admit it, but I think there is a silent, systemic level of discrimination when it comes to care-experienced young people. People like to be able to attribute dysfunctional behaviour to something, anything. You only have to watch the look of utter confusion on someone's face when gossiping about someone who had a wonderful childhood now battling addiction or mental health. They just can't understand it. How did they 'catch' an addiction when they had luxury family holidays and happily married parents?

I'm not in denial of the stats surrounding care-experienced crime, addiction or homelessness. That would be dangerous. It's vital to be aware of those stats so we can *do better*. What I'm advocating is allowing every care leaver to live in a society free from speculation, stigma or judgement. I've heard of a woman who had reached the highest position within one of the most respected services in the country, and it was only once she reached that position that she shared her care leaver status, for fear of never being given the opportunity in the first place. I was told her exact words were *'they would have only thought me unreliable and assumed I wouldn't turn up for work'*. What made her feel that would be the case? This being my book, I'm naturally looking to bring it back to myself. My first experience of a job interview after disclosing my care leaver status included the question *'Would you need any extra help with reading or writing?'*

Might send the interviewer a copy of this and sign it just to prove I can do big girl, joined-up handwriting too.

I've digressed but that was important.

Once you've handed your homework in, you need to list every child-friendly activity local to you, which would be a pretty simple task if you *had* children. Then comes the second most challenging of all the tasks: the eco map. A map of your entire support network, names, relationship distance between you and whether you would call upon them for long distance emotional support or in the immediate, physical sense. Again, to most this may seem like a simple activity. However, when most of your support network got swept away in the infertility tsunami and you had to do a stint inside the care system because there was no 'village' to pull upon, the eco map can prove a rather difficult task.

We actually found the relentless admin so stressful

we packed it all up and ran away to a friend's cottage in Cornwall for a weekend, hopeful that a change of scenery would help us to complete it all and meet our panel deadline. I loved that weekend. Wrapped in blankets next to a tiny woodburning stove, reading books, creating lists, talking while walking for miles, sharing our thoughts, hopes and anxieties. On reflection, that weekend together was one of the most beautiful and poignant of our relationship. Even I wasn't aware of it at the time but *that* was our moment. That intimate moment of pre-parenthood I'd longed for.

Those final 'just us' moments. The invisible equivalent of an expectant couple painting a nursery in dungarees together. You don't ever see or hear of weekends like that in the media or reflected within film or television. You never see a bump-less couple preparing for parenthood through the medium of paperwork or studying. There was something very raw about lying together in our thickest woollen jumpers discussing the unedited reality of attachment trauma, a child needing forever and just how much of a privilege it would be to have a young person look back at you one day and *believe* you to be just that. I'd come to discover those raw, unedited moments to be our journey's most precious nostalgia.

The Whatsup Group

No good process is complete without a bit of preparation training and that's exactly what we were about to embark on for four whole days. We were to go from feeling as though we were the only couple we knew hoping to be lucky enough to become parents through adoption, to meeting a whole bunch of other people equally hoping to become parents this way. It is adopters, you know, who are the 'lucky' ones, despite it so often being thought of as the child. There's still a bit of a skewed perception doing the rounds depicting adopters and the perceived amount of sun there must be shining from their nether regions. I'm as flawed as the next woman and can confirm, it's just your standard amount of sunshine peeking through the crack. I always felt that if motherhood came to me through this path, being granted the honour of parenting a child I had not carried but who could forever rest upon me until I can no longer breathe, would in return make me the luckiest woman alive.

I'm quite excited about the 'prep group' (as I'd

heard our social worker abbreviate it). I'd spent many an afternoon planning all the extra-curricular activities I and my new best friends would be getting up to, and had already taken the liberty of creating the WhatsApp group; I just needed the names to add to it. Every group needs strong, organised leadership. I'm more than happy to step up to the plate.

We arrive early; I want to make the right impression on my new friendship circle. Dependable. I've made a bit more than my usual effort appearance wise, giving the illusion that the last few years of trying to reach motherhood haven't taken quite the hair-thinning toll they actually have, and that I'm still very much up for cocktails. Albeit the hair may be finer, it's still very ready for letting itself down during the odd *mum night out*. We're one of the first to enter the training room, which is a good size with lots of windows. To the right of the door is a table laid out with mugs for tea and coffee alongside plates of biscuits and fruit. There's a large circle of school-style plastic chairs and a flip board at the front with three more of the green chairs positioned in a row directly to one side of it. Seated on one of the chairs is a very welcoming lady with short curly hair, wearing a skirt and soft red shoes. She has a load of booklets resting on her lap and a packet of flip chart pens positioned on the window ledge behind her. She asks for our names and if, when we've chosen our seats, we could write them on the stickers provided, making it easier for everyone to get to know each other.

We default to our natural behaviour when we're nervous and supposed to be sensible. Giggling. Whispering through sniggers on what immaturities we could write on our stickers and how many biscuits we could get away with taking home for later. The school-like feel to the room is not helping our behaviour. I only really excelled in dance and drama so to be reconciled with a flip chart in any capacity was enough to intimidate my non-studious youth, reverting me back to my pre-pubescent years of pratting around and rearranging my pencil case, mostly during maths. Just as I'm midway through reorganising my handbag, the door closes and the smiling lady stands up to introduce herself. She tells us a little bit about her role with the agency (turns out to be pretty big) and about what the next four days will entail (turns out to be rather a lot).

We go round the circle introducing ourselves one at a time, sharing what stage of the process we're currently in and if we're hoping to adopt one child or siblings. I place the partly organised bag back on the floor between my feet and sneak my hand underneath the protection of my husband's, like an out-of-place tortoise looking for its shell. I listen to everybody's name and personal journeys one by one; it's breathtaking. Up until today, we had only met one other couple who'd adopted, yet now we were sitting with quite literally a whole room full of potential adopters. There was something liberating in knowing over the next four days you would have someone other than your partner to talk to about the process. Of course, the few friends or family members who knew had shared an interest, checking in for updates, but *this* was different. It would mean not having to explain every intricate detail or abbreviated phrase in order for people to understand what you were even talking about. It meant you could simply talk. I don't think up until then I'd paid attention to just how isolating it had felt living through a process your immediate network isn't familiar with.

She takes no prisoners, this smiling, curly-haired, senior manager. Any sounds of nervous giggling and eagerly polite introductions are swiftly washed away with her reminding us all what the purpose of this group is: to gain more of an insight into what adoption *really* is. How the legal process works. What life as an adoptive parent is like and the scenarios of children who need adopting. She removes the lid from the top of a thick, green-nibbed pen and begins to create a list of all the reasons *we* believe a child may need to be adopted. It's an uncomfortable conversation to kick things off with. We're hardly all fighting to be the first to thrust our hands in the air. She's got little patience for coyness; this woman's here because she wants to make sure we've turned up for honest conversations. She's not interested in shying away from the grit; she needs to know we're capable and committed to talking about the harsh realities these children have had to face. After we've offered up a pitiful few reasons, she removes the lid from the red pen resting on the window ledge and, while turning her back to face the flip board, says:

'Your child will need to talk about their life, and it won't always be when you're prepared for it. It might be in the car or the supermarket. Showing them any uncomfortableness or bursting into tears every time could lead them to believe you're not OK to have those conversations.'

That was that. She'd whipped us all into shape with just two lids of a pen. By day over the next ninety-six hours, we really were only there to educate ourselves. By night, we would lie awake staring at walls and ceilings, unable to watch even reality TV because this subject held far more gravitas than I'd ever given respect to. I'd also be wording my email to Marvel, challenging their depictions of superheroes. Letting them know they could scrap the face paints and fancy capes because the kids I'd been hearing about were the real deal. Every new stat, lived experience story, textbook excerpt and professional insight only encouraged my feelings of *this* being how I wanted to become a mother. I wanted this to be my story, only it couldn't just be my book. It would be part of a trilogy; one I would be honoured to add my pages to. The triad is the official symbol for adoption, consisting of a heart surrounded by a triangle symbolising the birth family, the adoptive family and the adoptee. While lying awake feeling at times frightened, I also very much wanted to be a part of someone's triad.

During the tea breaks the personal conversations would happen, away from the prying ears of social workers who had no need to pry because they've heard it all already. There was a definite breaktime desire for most people to share their story, on the hunt for a bourbon and some relatable human connection. None of us fitted the commercialised marketing narrative of hopeful parents-to-be. There were couples who had tried treatment, some who never had. Same sex couples who only ever planned to adopt, heterosexual couples who only ever planned to adopt. Single individuals who hadn't yet met 'the one' (and would be damned if they were going to let a little thing like that get in the way of them becoming a parent). A couple with biological children wanting to expand their family, couples with no children hoping to grow theirs.

I don't know about you, but I really do think the 'market' would suit a little twenty-first-century glow-up. It's outdated, it's *always* been outdated, and it is predominantly women who face the pressure of living up to the stereotype. Starting long before you get married, with prams and tiny dollies. You certainly can't escape it once you get married. There's barely time to pick the confetti out of your hair before there are hopeful mutterings of a new heir to the semi-detached. It's everywhere, within films, TV, media and advertising. Smiling women with wonderful teeth, massive careers and expensive yoga pants. Good-looking husbands with a nice watch and strong jawline caressing bumps plastered across billboards. There's nothing wrong with that, I would love some expensive yoga pants. Of course, advertising agencies need to target the more saturated market, business is business. If you're not a part of that saturate, though, all it does is make you feel as though you don't 'fit in'. It's only very recently I've noted adverts reflective of same sex families and that relationship not being *the advert*. Just a family, going about family business while trying to sell us all a load of crap, as all good adverts should. The media seems to have finally grasped the fact that there are family units other than the OXO family, which gives me hope for a more inclusive future. I think making people feel as though they aren't visible is dangerous. Ensuring children grow up in a society seeing all family units represented is critical.

There were truths of early menopause, unexplained infertility, and not wanting to bring more children into the world when there are already many waiting for a further family. Honest tales of always knowing, wanting from the age of fifteen to adopt. Those who had arrived here after many years of trying and multiple losses. Second time adopters, and lovers who hadn't found each other until later in life. Partners who'd had a vasectomy, and an individual not wanting to take the risk of potentially passing down a genetic disorder. A single woman who raised an interesting point, one I'd certainly never considered, about the impact reproduction is having on the planet's resources. When faced with donor conception or adoption it was a thought (among many others) that helped make her decision. It's individual, personal, but we'd *all* arrived at this destination the same way we arrive anywhere. After a journey. However short or long, we'd all had one and it remains to this day an absolute honour to have been able to sit and hear of theirs, because wanting to start a family is a very personal decision. A rather private affair usually. The privilege of hearing another human being's story has never been lost on me.

Ironically, in many ways I had more deep-rooted similarities with individuals in that room than with most in our current support network. I didn't go rushing down to the nearest tattoo parlour, inking my wrist with their names, or giving out handmade friendship bracelets on departure day. I haven't remained in contact with any of them. The relationships didn't evolve into anything beyond the prep group and that was OK. I'd learnt that when you desperately want to be part of a tribe, you won't actually find one. Maybe you come across a bit too keen, like when I used to follow the popular timeshare kid round junior school to tell her I'd been to Butlins. It was too much, I should have hung back a bit, let her come to me. You may not always find your people in the places you assumed you would. A tribe can take you by surprise; they can form an eclectic mix. You could pick up new recruits in parks, through friends, work, or on the World Wide Web. Membership need not require them to have walked directly in your shoes. A willingness to try and understand can prove a strong foundation for new friendships to blossom after the grief of having lost too many.

The Cockroach and the Mouse

Both the dog and the cat proved not to be lunatics. Smoke alarms had been fitted with the very best batteries money could buy. The chimney had been swept, child locks fitted on every window and not one friend or family member had put them off taking us to the approval panel. All we had to do now was wait for our panel date and for our social worker to pull together a cracking PAR detailing every aspect of our life and all that had been asked of us over the past six months. (Bet she had a few sleepless nights trying to pull ours together by the deadline.) We had to sit tight one final time and wait for the date on which a room full of strangers would decide whether we would become parents or not.

This panel could be composed of independent experts. Social workers, a paediatrician, adoptive parents, those with experience of looked-after children and, most important of all, adoptees. It would be this collective holding the final decision. The one that would decide if I would *ever* hear a child call me *Mum*. This date really was the end of the road for us, we had nothing left to give. Our tanks had been running on fumes for a good while now. Should these individuals decide for whatever reason that this wasn't to be, it would be time to leave all dreams of reaching parenthood behind on the cutting room floor. I would die having never been granted the incomparable privilege of unconditionally loving a child. I would leave this earth having never lain beside a tiny sleeping body or brushed my finger across a sweaty little head. Picking up a child when they cried and holding them up even higher as an adult. *That* would be the love I wanted but would never get to know. This unspoken fear is a reality so many are faced with. Leaving this one life, having never been a mother. Not through choice, only pain.

I make my way into the panel room behind the armour of my husband's body, after three consecutive trips to the toilet. The clock on the wall immediately opposite me reads 11.30 a.m. It's the same room we sat in for our prep group training sessions, which offers a sense of familiarity at least. Only a few minutes in and I'm already sweating. I'd prepared for the inevitable wearing a pink sleeveless rollneck paired with dark blue denim jeans, leaving ample room for the pits to breathe. My neck, however, is shrivelling up like a tortoise. I have the epiphany in this room of why these tops are called turtlenecks. My husband has cracked out those nice shoes again, the same ones I noticed during a counselling session. (They've clearly become his *quest to fatherhood shoes*.) He looks nice, he always looks nice. He's wearing a navy jumper with a thick, mustard-yellow block strip along the bottom and a brown wax jacket. The jacket concerns me slightly. Out of the two of us, he most definitely perspires the most. I feel the grip of his hand underneath the table. I don't recall, in all the years he's held my hand, him ever holding it this tight. I use my uncrushed hand to reach for a glass of water. I'm trembling, the panel can all see I'm trembling; I pick up the empty glass and try to stop it from shaking with one of those 'don't show me up' stares. I also realise this is not the moment to look unstable so leave attempting to pour in the water and opt for another dry swallowing of saliva.

'*How are you both feeling?*'

The voice of the agency manager cuts across the trickling of water being poured into a glass for me by a panel member sitting to my right. There's a comforting look in the manager's eyes and a genuine level of care to her question. The instinctive act of kindness displayed by the lady pouring the water makes me feel a little more at ease.

We simultaneously try to clear our throats, which is not the most orchestral sound even from two people having registered themselves as non-smokers.

'*Nervous. We're both nervous.*'

What follows is a thirty-minute knockout round of questions. We've thrown ourselves back into the ring, donning our gloves for what can only be the final fight. Every member of the panel has something to ask us. Questions and answers rhythmically bounce back and forth between us and them, him and them, me and them, him and me. We knock questions out of the park when it comes to answering *why* we want to adopt and *how* we would best support a child having experienced loss, because they were expected and with any level of expectation comes a chance to prepare. We become each other's cornermen ready to step in if either one of us needs help. Just when we think we've done it, when we can feel the end of our parental title fight drawing to a close, we're asked a question we hadn't granted ourselves permission to ever *really* consider.

'*What are you looking forward to the most about becoming parents?*'

I watch those in the ringside seats eagerly look to us for our answer. I hear a faint ringing in my ears as I tentatively turn my head to face my husband. Everything has abruptly decelerated. The room and all objects within it start to slow down, even the water from the glass I'd now nervously knocked over is unable to trickle across the table as it should. It feels as though I'm looking at him in search of the answer of a lifetime. Our lifetime. From the night we first met on a sticky-floored nightclub the day Whitney Houston died, to every time he'd made me laugh, held my hand and kissed my head. The day we were told we couldn't conceive, eleven pink elephants, our Enid Blyton adventure, and the time I cried over a split teabag. Every holiday, duvet day and time spent bickering during food shops. For all the nights we'd dreamt of waking up to a little head peeping at us from behind our bedroom door and the longing for tiny cold toes nestling into our bed. The afternoon spent impersonating Miss Piggy and Kermit the Frog. For all the hours we didn't know if we would make it but really hoped we would, and for every bit of privacy we'd been robbed of in unjust defence of why we were childless. That's how long I look at his face, and when he tries to speak, he can't; he tries but it's too painful. The torment of answering the question he hadn't dared to ask himself hurts too much. He tries again through whimpers. I hear my six-foot-something beautiful soul of a man whimper like a tiny mouse pleading with the cat not to tease him. He rests his head in his hands and sobs. I watch the nape of his neck arch as he tries to make himself less visible, a weary mouse curling into a ball. A last-ditch attempt to escape the torment it's being subjected to and, if curling fails, he might play dead.

I don't want him to play dead. We are not dead. We're two people who fell in love and wanted to become a family. I am watching the deep-rooted pain behind how this question has made him feel, the hope he'd never allowed himself to have breaking him above anything else. Truthfully answering their question without words. It's with animalistic instinct I move my chair closer to his, pulling him in towards my chest, giving him the dignity of shielding his face from this room full of strangers because he has given enough, and I need him to know just how magnificent his fight has been. Mice approach other mice in pain, particularly the top mouse. I want him to know that, to me, he is the very top of all the mice. No matter the outcome or decisions that are to be made about us this afternoon. The only certainty is that I will *always* love this man. As we huddle together protectively wrapping our arms around one another like little pink tails, a voice gently washes over us.

'*I think you've answered our question.*'

It was over.

It ended somehow. We stand outside the door of the room that will decide our fate holding onto each other's hands. We follow the stranger gently coaxing us out of the cage into another room. We're weaved through desks, a coffee machine and office rooms with big glass windows before we reach our holding pen. A tiny room, bare, filled with only one chair and a desk. It's here we must wait until the panel chair tells us what will be. The only interesting thing about this room is its large square window, disproportionate to the size of the room.

I rest on a plastic chair. He, on the edge of a rectangular desk. There's space between the chair and the table for us to reach across and hold hands. For this comfort, I start to think the room a work of architectural genius.

I notice his shoes touching mine. My shoes always look crap compared to his. He nurtures his far better than I do. Keeps them in the boxes, invests in shoe trees and the correct shade of polish. I really ought to start doing that. If this decision comes down to footwear, it won't be his that let the side down. We occasionally stare into each other's eyes but don't really speak. I suppose there isn't really anything left to say today.

I'd become familiar with disappointment; I could set my watch by it. My first experience of heartache came unsuspectingly from my parents when it really should have been some spotty, teenage boy. Then came all the usual bits, realising you weren't as fantastic as your cocky nineteen-year-old self had had you believe. The world not thinking you're the next best thing since sliced bread. You're just another slice of bread. Some will skip through with theirs buttered, some won't. Some end up in a training flat with neighbours proclaiming how they're going to set fire to you in your bed one sunny Sunday afternoon, some won't.

Some people meet someone, fall in love, get married and start a family. As straightforward as that. Others spend half a decade of their life trying, develop chronic hives, take scratchy sabbaticals, and dedicate months to a very intense process in a bid to reach motherhood. It's a part of this thing called life. Something you can never really prepare for, yet we're all here to live it. There was a time I hurt, beyond what words allow me to describe, but it's hard to still feel the weight of that pain when you now know a love so beautiful there aren't words vast enough to describe it.

Although you're led to believe by your social worker that you wouldn't be taken to panel unless they were pretty certain you would be approved, it's still only 'pretty certain', isn't it? Knowing that and everything at stake, you can't wait in this room without fear of them saying no.

The last few months of this process hadn't wholly been about me. Every moment of reflection had included the fight to reach a child who could be out there, fighting to get to me. The cockroach sits quietly staring out of an inaccurately scaled window thinking of the child who could be waiting. The one who could be sitting on a swing with the sunshine on their face wrapped in a temporary love from foster carers. A child who could be sleeping in a different cot or bed today from yesterday's. One who may have hugged a sibling for the final time in childhood. Asked to separately climb aboard journeys towards unknown destinations.

It is here, staring out of this ridiculous pane of never-ending glass, I go against everything I'd always believed was a load of old hogwash, wholeheartedly asking the universe to make damn sure that the panel chair comes back in here and allows us a shot to find each other in this lifetime. All previous feelings of 'trusting in the system' have gone out the window because this is serious now. This comes down to giving a child their *right* to consistent love, support, respect, loyalty and advocacy from a couple who would feel privileged beyond words to give it, so I don't care how many degrees this woman's got or how many times she's won employee of the month – when she comes back inside this room I'm socking it to her, good and proper.

'*Hello.*'

I keep my head to the floor.

'*Sorry we've taken a little while.*'

I need a reason not to look at her so pretend my shoelace has come undone.

'*We are all in agreement, this was a unanimous decision today.*'

I can't steady my fingers enough to lift the tip of the lace from the floor.

'*We think you would make wonderful parents.*'

—

Silence.

Silent.

Nothing.

My mind replaying her words.

Parents.

We think . . .

Parents.

My arm reaches up for her hand.

I squeeze my palm into hers.

The weight of my neck won't allow me to lift my head.

Smiling.

I hear my husband thanking her, for the *belief*, the *chance*.

They've given us new life by *entrusting* us with some-one else's.

Smiling.

I see his knees and feel his arms around my waist.

I listen to him whisper, '*We did it.*'

I feel his hands on my ears as he lifts my head.

My neck softens.

What Makes a Mum?

She leaves.
We stay.
We hold.
We stay.
We breathe.
We cry.
We breathe.
We breathe.
We can breathe.
We are not dead.

URLs, Parades and Filters

I've noticed people quite enjoy sharing their conception memoirs. Especially with young people. This could be because they think it a really beautiful moment, or they quite enjoy the look of total embarrassment displayed across a wrinkle-free face. Maybe it's egos needing others to know they *were* lusted after and most definitely 'at it' during their lifetime. My all-time favourite is a postman's first-born conception memory, offered up to us while on our doorstep. I won't ever be able to watch a Christmas parade in the same light again (which is fine, as I've never been to one). Christmas parades aside, there are many other experiences, less conventional, very early stages of pre-parenting you never really hear about. Which is strange because every parent in effect becomes a mother or father to a child they've never met. I think some diversity in these experiences would prove useful in 2024.

You don't hear many stories about people finding their child on a website, do you? Not such a widely understood experience that one. People might be able to get their head around the Christmas parade

(I'm still trying to), but having to log on to a platform night after night, applying 'filters', which are basically technological tools, to assist you in trying to find a suitable match? Most would just look at you in shock. My significant others did, anyway.

It's not a nice story, is it, applying software to profiles of human beings.

Children.

That's how it was.

That's how it still is.

I found it incredibly uncomfortable. This is a website containing profiles of too many children needing permanence and security. Basic human rights we might take for granted. Pictures of children next to a few words. Some have a half-decent picture, a video even and words written with a great deal of detail and care. Others less so. Sometimes because of safeguarding issues, others because of a lack of resources, so I'd been told.

Behind the photographs, gender, likes and dislikes, age, ethnicity, developmental milestones and any known health conditions lies the heartbreaking undertone. Children, unknowingly on a website, needing adults to love and care for them.

It's everything that's wrong with the world, where such a well-deserved opportunity of hope is tangled together with URLs, buttons and filters. A resource designed to bring human beings together but lacking any human contact at all. It's important to stress, of course, that this is a secure page to which you can only gain access once approved to adopt.

Once you log in, you're immediately met with your personal profile page containing your picture and words describing you. It's not an easy photo to choose; an image that implies you'd make good parents isn't a genre of photography I'd come up against before. We went for us both standing in front of a model of a giant diplodocus wearing outfits showing we're 'on trend' but practical. I'm flashing my pearly whites (still reaping the benefits of that tooth whitening session). He looks friendly, dependable and kind. Neither of us looks insane. Overall, we felt it was our best shot. Literally. Your profile sits on there as a prospective parent, alongside many others. Potentially, your child's profile is floating in there among a sea of beautiful others too. Somewhere between that and the filter key, you need to find each other.

So, there you have it. Our very early pre-parenting memoirs. Logging onto a laptop trying to find our child, and I'm not knocking the process because what other way is there to do it? Is there ever going to be a prettier way to find further family for children waiting in an oversubscribed, underfunded care system? For a start, they're in the care system. There's really nothing very pretty about that.

I have just one request for those with a level of responsibility on this website, those whose job it is to represent and create profiles for children and those responsible for responding to prospective adopters. Remember at the very heart of it, on either side, sit human beings. A poorly taken photograph, misspelt words, inaccurate information or replying only with 'not suitable' or 'considering another match' doesn't really reflect that reality.

The consequence of cutting funding, reducing resources and loading up social workers with more caseloads than is viable will inevitably result in no or poor responses to adopters and children's profiles lacking the corporate parental care, accuracy, advocacy and respect with which they should only ever be presented.

Miniature Spiderthem

I need you to understand this: I believe I have a duty of care, as I write this book, to the hundreds of profiles we saw during the adoption process and the information we read. You're talking about people's lives here, not the edited, drowning in filters versions people flood their social media profiles with (we've all done it), but the raw, unedited truths and, at times, harrowing facts documenting the start of people's lives.

I don't believe anyone has the right to unnecessarily share an adopted child's history. Although the many profiles we saw were not those of our child, they will forever have my utmost respect. That's just how it is.

I think I expected to log on to Link Maker (the national website where approved adopters are able to view the profiles of children) and be immediately floored by a profile of our child. I mean, you hear the God-awful stats, you know there are far too many children in the care system, so this next part of the process should be an absolute doddle. We'd made it through the tough part, filled out every form under the sun and repeatedly topped up the smoke alarms with new batteries. Surely this was it?

WRONG.

That rather naïve thinking was incorrect on many levels, by the way, because this process is never really about finding the right child for a family. It's about finding the right family for *the child*. Any focus on the ratio is irrelevant.

Are you the right person/s to guide this human being through the rest of their life?

This is the only question that really matters and the answer to that won't be in your hands.

See, I told you this wasn't going to be easy.

My logical head reminds me how I knew it wouldn't be that simple; we'd been forewarned umpteen times throughout assessment that family finding is the hardest part of the process. My right brain (the unrestricted part) says, *remember you didn't really take that bit in, you didn't want to*. Of course, the truth of this was, I'd been so focused on arriving here, getting approved, hearing someone say after all these years that there was actual genuine hope of me becoming a mother, there really wasn't much headspace beyond that to think of the brutality of family finding.

Then came the learnings and greater levels of understanding about family finding we'd gained throughout assessment. The parts no one really talks about. Our family finders (that is an actual job title) had no qualms in telling us from the outset that babies aged from nought to twelve months were the most sought-after. This is predominantly because adopters have concerns around attachment and attachment trauma, believing it may be easier to create or overcome with a much younger child.

Nancy Newton Verrier, psychotherapist, adoptive parent and author of *The Primal Wound: Understanding the Adopted Child*, elaborates on the Primal Wound Theory surrounding early infancy adoption which has been said to 'revolutionise how we think about adoption'.

I'm no psychotherapist. All I have to offer are my personal insights gleaned along the assessment way and it's these I share in hope of a more informed society.

The biggest personal awakening of all?

The painful reality that any child, having suffered the loss of a birth family, has consequently experienced a level of trauma.

You could be an hour or ten years old.

It's a trauma.

And it damn well matters.

For me, reaching motherhood was never about the desire for a baby. It was about becoming a mother. Raising a child.

Another matching conversation no one really wants to have is the uncomfortable task of deciding what you are *hoping for* in a match and your *realistic capabilities*. If you've been approved as suitable adopter/s for one, two, three or more children, how do you then find your child or children out of the thousands waiting? The brutal reality is there are thousands of children in the system, but you're not adopting thousands of children. How you reach that decision is through the education and training provided by your voluntary adoption agency or local authority, enabling more informed (and crucially) *honest* conversations with your partner and/or yourself throughout your own personal journey.

The process teaches many things, a great deal of which reflect upon yourself.

I think the honest questions any prospective adopter should be asking themselves are:

Is the level of information I have here before me enough?

Could I support this child or these children for the rest of my life?

Is there any doubt in my mind that I may not be able to do that?

These children aren't looking for anyone to 'save them' (whatever that's even supposed to mean). *They* throw *you* the life raft anyway, trust me. They deserve the critical simplicities we all deserve: unconditional, unwavering and consistent love. Someone flying their flag from the highest corner every single day regardless of uncertainties that may lie ahead.

So, after the uncomfortable conversations with myself and with my husband, *why* was I still sobbing into my pillow each night having moved no further forward along this family finding path?

Because family finding is just not that simple, that's why, and after the journey of family finding reflection, forms, assessments and security passwords comes the need for an intrinsic human connection.

From across the screen.

Not. Easy.

No one wants to get this wrong. Not you, or the social workers, family finders, foster carers, courts, judge and, above everyone else, the child. Not one person wants a 'disruption', the term used to formally describe an adoption placement breaking down and the child or children being placed back into foster care. Tragically, even with all the training, under-standing, honesty and best intentions in the world, disruptions still happen. My jaw nearly hit the floor when our social worker spoke of disruptions, as this had never occurred to me. I hadn't allowed myself to think about it. An ironic mindset, given that I was living in receipt of a biological maternal disruption. Of course, disruptions aren't unique to adoption and can happen within birth families. I would hazard a guess at that being particularly prevalent in the teen-age years. I guess it was the added layer of tragedy when it came to thinking of an adoption breaking down, knowing these children had already lost so much before they even came to being adopted. Though most disruptions occur during the secondary school years (a potential concern/fear for adopters), many happen within the first six weeks of placement. There are no official UK statistics as families are under no obligation to keep local authorities and agencies updated once adoption orders are granted and children leave their care. It is thought between

4 per cent and 11 per cent of UK adoptions end in a disruption.[12]

Hard fact to stomach, that one.

A heartbreaking reality for *all* involved.

This is the biggest decision you will ever make in your life; one you may never have anticipated making and one no other life choice will ever come close to in terms of its gravity. These children show the tenacity of human life in its most vulnerable of forms because *many* have survived immeasurable loss before they've even tried on their first pair of school shoes.

Little heavyweight champions of the world.

So when the prep group WhatsApp was popping off left, right and Chelsea with news of matches, linking and panels, I never compared my journey to theirs, and if this is your life stage right now, I urge you to do the same. Stay in your own lane, keep driving and never take your foot off the gas to draw comparisons. We won't all get there on the same road; that's why the Spaghetti Junction was built.

The reality is (as I've heard from many prospective adopters) you may fully understand the gravitas, find a profile you really believe could be the one, feel a connection from across the screen, be desperate for more information and, as much as you sensibly try not to (and at this stage are contradictorily advised not to) emotionally invest, you can't help but think about the possibility of loving and advocating for this child for the rest of your life. So, you click on the big red button at the top of the page reading 'show interest' and wait.

Wait.

You wait.

Refresh the page.

Wait.

And about six weeks later you get a response (if you're lucky) reading:

Stronger matches available.

Family finding newsflash. YOU can be rejected, gang! Yes, *YOU* with the stable career, long-term relationship, semi-detached with south-facing garden and numerous coffee loyalty cards can very much be rejected. This had been the story for many in our prep group. You might finally find what you believe to be the right profile, after months, maybe even years, of searching. The only thing left to do now is tell the child's social worker you're all set before rushing to the shops to buy every single clothing item in your soon-to-be-child's size because you've cracked it, and what else could there possibly be left obstructing the way between you and your future child now?

Social workers, that's what.

It is the child's representative that will have the final say in this situation, not you. Just as you may have your criteria, they have theirs and it is *they* who will decide, regardless of your thoughts on the matter, if the 'interest' is to proceed any further. You may get feedback, although you probably won't. There's no time or resources to give constructive criticism to the many who are of no interest when they need to start working through the ones who are. That's just family finding business and I want to be honest with you because there wasn't (and still isn't) enough honesty around, it's cut-throat.

I don't disagree with the reality of the child's representative holding the final decision, acting only in the best interests of the child. I understand and accept as the fully grown adult it's not really about me and how I may be feeling. But when I hear about local authorities wanting to hold onto money so they won't look at placing a child out of their paid geographical area irrespective of how strong the match could potentially be, I can't help but question the ethical values of the social care system.

It was during our family finding phase that we were told of the other family finding resources (as they called it) available to us. These methods were referred to as 'profiling events' and 'activity days'. Profiling events consist of approved adopters bringing along a handful of one-page profiles about themselves. I've tried to dress it up for you but it's basically a flyer of yourself, a miniature billboard if you will, highlighting only your very best selling points. The aim is for you to make a connection with a child's social worker or representative away from the restrictions of computer screens, with the opportunity to hand out some of these 'strut cards' making it impossible for said social workers to forget you, possibly bearing you in mind for any future potential matches. Be warned, however: the paper grade can become highly competitive, with some prospective adopters splashing out on high gloss

200 gsm flyer material while the less experienced among us merely print them out at home on your average sheet of A4.

At profiling events there are also paper profiles of children waiting to be matched, in the hope of prospective adopters taking a copy if they feel there could be a connection. I remember the very first time I touched a paper profile of a child. The feel of the sheet, the weight of its corner as I uncomfortably peeled it away from the stack it was lying on. The crisp whiteness behind the photo and the words written underneath. I read every word twice, possibly three times, and from that moment on I vowed never to pick up a profile of a human being from a stack of paper and not give them the dignity of time. Always reading the brief words offered, staring into their eyes even just for a few seconds, wanting them to know, regardless of any decisions, that they as individuals, as children, not 'profiles', had been *seen*.

Family finding isn't for the faint-hearted. It's made clear from the outset that your emotions are way down the pecking order. In fact, they're barely on it. Another reason why a period of grief between ending treatment (if that's been your journey) and starting the process is advised. If you need therapy or emotional support of any sort, invest in it beforehand because you won't be getting a whole lot once you start this part of the process. During this stage, you're expected to morph into some sort of family finding robot, unfazed by the two- or three-word response to your expression of interest. Remain positive during the months, even years, passing you by while you wait. Take the lack of compassionate responses on your metal chins after professionals have read documents detailing the most private aspects of your life before notifying you as to whether you're being considered or not. I know this to be the case because I hear it time and time again from prospective adopters, and while nothing can be done to ease the waiting for a match, the way prospective adopters' emotions are at times disregarded during this stage of the process is concerning.

The system sort of expects it all from you by this point. You want to invest in a child you haven't yet met, hoping to love and support them for the rest of their life; you understand the seriousness of the process and make considered choices before you even go so far as to press that red button, but then you get a no. Or it's been two months without a response and no sign of one ever coming. Then you're expected never to have allowed yourself to invest that much at all, to dust yourself off, get back out there and do it all over again.

There are parts of the process I feel prospective adopters could be *significantly* more supported through. People should be granted the dignity of a response; agencies shouldn't continue to approve adopters if they know the current ratio of adopters to children is unequal; councils shouldn't make financially led placement decisions over child-centred ones. Equally there are parts to this that really ought not to be about the adopters at all. To put it bluntly, it shouldn't be about feeling sorry for yourself through-out this. You won't be able to anyway, even on the days you really want to, because you're surrounded by some of the most inspirational superheroes of all time. Nothing offers grounding and a reminder that this is not actually entirely about you like some of this country's most inspirational young people.

I developed a social worker girl crush during one of these profiling events, like one you might have on your favourite female pop star. I'd gone out to the refresh-ment area on a mission to eat my feelings with a slab of homemade chocolate cake. I'd just taken a giant bite of self-pity after announcing how difficult and desperately sad it all was reading these children's pro-files. The social worker standing next to me offered me not even so much as a raise of an eyebrow while continuing to strain her teabag on the edge of her cup; only words, and ones I didn't ever want to forget:

'I'm afraid it's not half as hard for you as it is for the children.'

Now that reaction might not please everyone and I admit, in that exact moment with a puffy, tear-covered face full of chocolate cake and my mouth falling ever so slightly ajar, I doubt I looked all that grateful to be in receipt of it either, but it was the right pep talk for me. I needed a reality check, a bit of tough love, what-ever you want to call it. How was I going to find my child if I kept crying, falling into pits of sadness some-times lasting days as I secretly had been? I needed to keep my gloves on and stay focused – I owed it to the child who had no choice but to be wearing theirs. She won't actually ever know, that tea-straining professional, but she became the Mickey Goldmill to my inner Rocky that afternoon, accountable for the family finding coaching session I didn't know I needed. It would be nice to see a few more social workers celebrated. Someone has to have the ability to stick to the facts, professionally plough on through, separate themselves from the emotion of it all while best supporting these children. We can't all be blowing into a hankie every two minutes – that's no sodding use to anyone.

She'd been round the old matching block a bit, that one, seen many a prospective adopter having a crack at making it all about how they were feeling. I think she knew exactly what she was doing that day and I'm very glad she did because that one sentence encouraged me to dig deeper than I'd ever dug before and try to find the child we were meant to bring home.

Our social worker had informed us about 'activity days'. We were told these events usually consisted of 'harder to place children'. I feel sick writing that sentence. When I heard of a charity that had not felt all that comfortable with the phrase either, instead opting for 'children who wait the longest', it highlighted to me the vital importance of language. How the improvement in advocacy needed for those in the system should start right from the very beginning, with the basic language that professional services choose to use. There will be future adult children of the system reading they were 'hard to place'. Who even signed that phrase off? It's basic stuff, isn't it?

How can we ask better of society when it comes to understanding the care system when the language from within it isn't all that great?

Children who wait the longest: sibling groups, children over the age of three, male, from an ethnic minority background or having mental or physical disabilities. The 'activity day', as I understood it, gave the children an opportunity to 'step off the page', have their laughter heard, imaginations admired, and their sheer bravery respected. This put a little bit of 'human' back into a process that was otherwise uncomfortably disconnected. It also gave us prospective adopters the opportunity to look beyond our laptops, a chance to potentially rethink our initial search criteria. We met real life superheroes that day, not the Marvel comic book types with their fictional superpowers. These wonderful children, with their *invisible* superpowers, were far greater than them all.

We had something in common, all of us, no matter how old: we *all* hoped to find forever. There was something strikingly beautiful and painfully sad about that.

We walked in. There was a friendly face at a large table to the right of the foyer who asked for both our names, looked down at her list, ticked us off and asked us to write our names on those white sticky labels you had to use on school trips. She explained how the children would also be wearing a sticker, only theirs would have a number indicating how many siblings they had or whether they were an only child. The walls were plastered with the creative works of little minds. The carpet leading into the sports hall where the event was taking place was practical. I'm odd like that; no matter what the situation, I'm guaranteed to both notice and have an opinion on the interior.

To the right of the hall entrance was a large, disabled toilet; the door had been left ajar and I could see the red emergency cord dangling down. As I turned my head back to the practical carpet, I nearly tripped over a miniature Spiderthem rushing towards us, playing chase with another child. I could hear laughter, innocence.

I noticed Spidie's sticker.

2.

I immediately forgot the earlier pep talk from my social worker crush and with tears frantically about to escape ran to hide them in the toilet. A rather flustered-looking husband bundled in behind. I was half expecting him to remind me of the chocolate cake chat, start telling me to get it together, but he looked pretty bloody affected by the short experience himself, and we hadn't even made it into the room yet. We'd been prepped for this day, attended an earlier meeting explaining the format, received guidance on the conversations and questions we could find ourselves being asked:

'Are you going to be my new mummy and daddy?'
Or
'Am I coming home to live with you now?'

If you haven't stepped inside the world of adoption, this will prove hard to believe, no doubt, but these briefings are happening in corporate settings up and down the country. What not to say to a child asking if you're going to be their parent. How to deflect the question of am I moving in with you next. It sounds fabricated almost, an author's attempt to tug at the old heartstrings in a bid to get you all to marvel at the emotion of their writing. Only there is a *no literacy talent needed* disclaimer to this book. I need not fabricate any of it. This is real life; this really is happening. Children are in a system waiting for families, at events, wearing stickers asking strangers if they could be the ones to love them. These conversations happen and they will be happening again this week and the week after that. This is why this book matters – because some people reading won't know, and if we don't know, *how* can we endeavour to stand up and do better, advocate for better, be it politically, empathetically or inclusively? The media like to use the phrase 'current care crisis', don't they? I'm sure we've all heard it bandied around, possibly with the intention to shock a government into caring. Only it's been flung around for so long now, I fear it's provoked an immunity to the severity of the crisis. And there's nothing 'current' about it: the care system has been in crisis for decades.

You only have to look at the once in a generational opportunity the government had recently been given to step up and implement change in response to the independent review of children's social care in 2022. £2.6 billion was the recommended amount needed to overhaul the current system. Only what this actually meant was the government needing to open the purse strings. They offered less than 10 per cent of what had been advised for children who are reliant upon a parental government until they can be heard.[13] The British Association of Social Workers (BASW) England said, 'the proposals appeared unlikely to deliver the funding needed to tackle the urgent crisis in children's social care'. While a major children's charity responded, 'they're effectively putting over 82,000 children in care at the bottom of the pile. The £200 million announced today won't even scratch the surface.'[14] For financial context, I remember watching the news shortly after this shameful response and discovering how Bradford council alone spent £100 million in a year. I recently read this is forecasted to reach £242 million in 2023.[15]

You could argue that the responsibility falls wider than this. I suppose there is an argument to suggest that while children are being cared for by the state, they're being cared for by us all. So, when we see or hear of such pitiful responses, what's stopping any one of us from challenging these decisions? The same way any parent would for a child. Could this *care crisis* be the nation's responsibility?

We re-emerged from the toilet, neither one of us having given the other a pep talk. We had a little hug, flushed a few soggy tissues down the loo and agreed to just get back out there and enjoy the privilege of these wonderful kids' company for a few hours.

We rode trikes, played table football, laughed, learnt how to play a wooden frog instrument. My husband fully committed to the glitter face painting table (any excuse). I seriously underestimated how small the elastic backs are on a children's pair of fairy wings leaving myself rocking the one-winged butterfly look for the foreseeable, before finding myself being locked away for one hundred million years by the miniature Spiderthem, only allowed to escape if I were to use the spider force trike to go to Asda and buy the younger sibling some nappies.

There we have it, ladies and gentlemen. A very real example of the adult levels of compassion these children possess. For a few precious moments a child portrays their favourite superhero, immersed in a world of high-steepled towers, energy balls and fire-breathing dragons. Only there's a part of them instinctively left sitting on the childhood side-lines for their sibling. The need to know they will be OK, basic needs will be met. This superhero can't grant themselves permission to *only* play make-believe; that entitlement has been stolen.

I want you to know how incredible you are. The child with the webbed Lycra face, who I spent no more than a couple of hours with. *You* and your miniature sidekick. Fighting crime, saving cities and stockpiling nappies. You need not don another hero's suit, *yours* surpasses them all.

You inspired me more than any tutor, CEO or politician has over the years.

One of my life's greatest pleasures, you locking me in that dungeon.

An absolute honour and a downright privilege.

NASA Training and Cuban Cigars

Days rolled into weeks; months evolved into more hours staring at a computer screen. Only instead of remaining solely focused on family finding, we'd expanded to *all-inclusive* searching, seeking a break from the monotony of nothingness and empty inboxes, and developing a new habit of hitting the refresh button. I wanted to escape the nightly shuffling past an empty little bedroom. It's a crime to wish your life away, but I couldn't help committing that crime when it came to hoping days, hours and minutes passed as quickly as possible while waiting for a match.

We did what most on this relentless journey to parenthood do. Fill the painful void with 'stuff' – anything will do. Hobbies you don't want, events you don't care about, and tediously long books you never reach the end of. We opted for a holiday; we figured we bloody well deserved one and thought we could wash down the uncertainty of it all with a mojito and a freshly rolled Cuban cigar. Gives you something to focus on, a vacation. Especially if you factor in a good few months' 'planning time', deliberating over how many plug adapters to pack and the best fake tan to use. I can now professionally advise on hobbies not to begin (Zumba) and impart how any fake tan will make your knees look like a couple of cheesy Wotsits, regardless of the online reviews.

We were extremely 'lucky' to be able to cry abroad that summer; that with me now having returned to work for almost a year and the infertility debt slowly being chipped away, we could wait anxiously on a beach somewhere instead. Although we were *approved to be parents*, not a lot was happening, and tears don't sting as much if you've had to use a passport. (This is sarcasm and not to be taken as advice; they still very much sting.) Only, holidays for childless couples come with a social clause. Misconceptions from colleagues, acquaintances, and anyone else who granted themselves a permit to announce how 'lucky' we were to be going on holiday without kids, cut even deeper than the 'at least you have a nice house' statements. People didn't seem to understand that you book the adults-only hotel because the thought of hearing children laughing in the sun, splashing water and screaming 'no' at bottles of sun cream would only leave you on a lounger silently crying behind your shades.

Ask yourselves: are the couple who have devoted half a decade, sometimes even multiple decades, of their life to trying to reach parenthood really as 'lucky' as you may have yourselves believe?

Since writing this book I've developed a genuine

distaste for the word 'lucky'. We either need to start a more appropriate, regulated use of it or just cross it out of the dictionary. (This is why I would never make it as a world leader – too power hungry.)

Planning through loss became an inherent life skill of mine. I've used planning to survive. I'm rather spectacular at it. Bear Grylls would advise you to drink your urine; I would always encourage scheduling every aspect of your life. I've always been very responsible (apart from that one time I got engaged on a Spanish island), not to be confused with boring. I can get my groove on all night long on a single bottle of Evian and a Tic Tac. Never tried a drug, never felt the need. Not remotely curious.

I wasn't a spontaneous player as a child, I liked some order to my games, a bit of structure. Coincidentally, one of my favourite playtime memories is me packing a lunchbox suitcase for a holiday. Sitting on the aeroplane stairs sucking an extra-strong mint I'd nabbed out of my dad's coat pocket, then unpacking all my worldly goods (a Tamagotchi and a half-eaten jelly baby) at the Playa del hallway. I'd made a passport and paper money in *both* currencies just in case I ran into any issues. I was eighteen when I first went on a real aeroplane (that's why I accepted the proposal – Canary Island jetlag). I remember a girl at school who always had the best of everything, like cheese strings. Epitome of middle class, the cheese string. You knew you weren't off the council estate if you were peeling back bits of cheese and had one of those flip-up pencil cases with a built-in sharpener. She would regularly come back from 'the time share' with a colourful braid in her hair. I thought she was well posh and used to follow her round (partly hoping for a bit of cheese) but mainly because I thought she was everything I wasn't.

I've spent quite a lot of my life feeling embarrassed, ashamed even. Embarrassed for being a care leaver, growing up skint, embarrassed my mother was ill and my dad an alcoholic. I carried this great level of shame around with me and assumed being posh, having access to cheese strings or a braid, meant you would be accepted. I had a lot of pre-conceived ideas about perfection as a child. That's what makes children so vulnerable, isn't it? I would fantasise, correct people on the pronunciation of my council estate and at times avoid the humiliation of standing in childhood's line of disadvantage, the free school meal queue, opting for an afternoon of tummy rumbling instead. Who the hell came up with that open approach to bullying? Here we go, kids, one line for the poor and one for the cheese peelers. Please form an orderly non-piss-taking queue.

My perceptions are reformed now: I'll take up an offer of a free meal any day of the week and am fiercely, book-worthy proud of my beginnings. I ended up earning a place at one of Britain's most prestigious drama schools because I wanted to act, and when I told my dad about this ambition, he said I had to go for the best because why shouldn't I? So, I did, and I got in. Only, I very nearly didn't because I didn't have any credit to listen to the multiple voicemails on my phone from the receptionist offering me the place. They tracked me down in the end, so I handed the keys of my care leaver council flat back to my support worker and off to Hollywood I skipped. My dad always let it be known to me from a very young age that with education and a passion there is *possibility*, regardless of social or economic background. It was important to him that I believed that; he said it with an equal amount of conviction when drinking or sober. His message always remained consistent, and this is an important point I'm trying to make here because, although he couldn't always be consistent in the practical parenting sense, the power in his constant instillation of self-belief had a profound impact on me as a developing person. Had I told him I wanted to be an astronaut he would have researched which National Diploma would get me to NASA.

The day I started my training there (drama school, not NASA), he walked me up to the entrance, held my hand and cried.

I had lessons in received pronunciation, quite a lot and a few extra over lunchtimes. I loved acting, dancing and felt alive whenever I set foot on stage. It did grant possibility, but I never felt as though I fitted in. I never felt *good enough, elite enough*. The same imposter syndrome I'm challenging by writing this book. I've always loved anything creative but felt a bit misplaced doing it. Acting, writing a novel, pottery. I like all of it (with the exception of the pottery), but you can enjoy doing something and still feel like you don't belong. In my very first week a fellow student asked if I'd ever been to the 'National'. I didn't even know what that was, so replied 'no'; he just stared at me like I had my arse stuck on my head.

I've come to realise dysfunction exists above the breadline, below it, or if you're next in line to the throne. If it's there, it's there, and the story of a vulnerable young mother, spending her days walking round a shopping centre with a toddler and a newborn because it was warm while a vulnerable young father went off to work until the hostel they were living in opened again, now fills me with pride because it means I've come from grit and it's this grit and determination to keep fighting that propped me up during my quest to reach motherhood.

In the weeks preceding the booking of our tropical painkiller, we'd discovered a little person far more captivating than any picture of turquoise waters and vibrant streets.

I'm downstairs watching television. My husband must be shouting with great gusto because I can hear every syllable he's saying above the volume. I think I *know* what he could be talking about but don't want to allow myself any hope. Although this is difficult because I know he's probably upstairs family finding (one of us usually was) and I hadn't yet heard him show *this* level of enthusiasm. I pause the programme to compose any hope of the child I imagine he could be talking about before placing the remote gently on the coffee table. I wait until the base of the remote touches the wood before tentatively tying the belt of my dressing gown.

'*You need to get up here* now.'

I run, leaving a trail of white fluffy belt behind me.

As I burst through the semi-open door of our bedroom, I'm struck by the animation beaming from my husband's eyes. There's a definite sprinkling of excitement scattered in each of his pupils. He's sitting upright against the headboard of our bed, the laptop balancing on his outstretched legs. His hands are cupping each side of the screen, protective of what it is he can see. He's smiling. I've not seen him smile this truthfully in far too long.

Only what he has seen, what he is about to show me has allowed him this smile. He delicately releases one hand from the screen and moves the laptop to face me.

'*Look.*'

Before I can find the courage to look, I look at my husband once more, with an unbelted dressing gown and pyjamas way past their sell-by date standing on our bedroom floor among bedside tables, a tilted lampshade and odd socks strewn across the floor. Internally pleading to *let this child be the one*.

He signals for me to sit beside him and points to the child on the screen.

In a lifetime there will be very few moments of which you will remember every intricate detail. This will eternally be one of mine. When we learnt of a human being so remarkable and read words about a little person so inspiring, you understand what it is to be spellbound. The day we sat looking at a screen and felt a child's soul shining back at us.

The spellbinding spirit of an individual we only dared *hope* to walk, dance and sit beside.

Forever.

Each tiny finger leaves me yearning to grab hold of his hand, envious of the toy he's holding. There's an instinctive desire to reach my hand through the laptop and pull the tiny striped sock hanging off his little foot up over his ankle for fear of his toes feeling the cold or tripping over when he tries to stand.

I read all there is to read, every word, each like and dislike. What it is that makes him laugh and what makes him frown. I so desperately want to laugh and frown beside him. I read about his bedtime routine, what he likes to eat, how old he is, and with every word it becomes harder to suppress any feelings of excitement and hope, now that we have learnt about him. Any attempts at suppression are made impossible with my husband repeating every word that's been written, excitedly pointing, and underlining each sentence with his finger just to ensure I've seen it. I would be well informed even if I haven't because he is practically shouting them all out again.

Late that night we try the ritual of going to bed but can't sleep. We recite all we have learnt about the little boy who has captivated us both. The one snuggled up in a bed somewhere we don't know, being cared for by people we have never met. Tonight, all we can do is lie side by side staring up to the ceiling that had taunted us so often and wait to speak to our social worker in the morning.

Until then, we whisper him a *goodnight*.

We're pacing around hours before the acceptable UK time to make a phone call of 9 a.m. We try our luck at 8 a.m., only it appears our social worker has a life, so it goes straight to voicemail. I skip breakfast in favour of another look at his picture before I have to hit the road and get to work. My husband and I discuss the social worker contact strategy over cold coffees, which basically consists of both of us trying to pin her down at any available opportunity throughout our working days. We conclude that it would become acceptable to withhold our number if we felt our phone calls weren't top of her priority list *and*, if we'd had no luck by 4 p.m., sending a 'This is an emergency' text was also entirely justified. We give each other a nervous, fumbling kiss goodbye and a reminder to make contact as soon as either of us has any news.

I jump in the car, check the Bluetooth is working and my phone is on charge. The clock reads 8.45 a.m.; I should have left a good fifteen minutes earlier but remain unfazed. I'd been promoted again despite the sabbatical due to my child-free, perceived married to the organisation status, so who was going to give me a telling off really? On any normal day I'd have my Grime, R'n'b and musical theatre ballads blasting from the sound system but not today. Today, I refuse to even have the radio on low for fear of missing a call or becoming distracted by my traffic light popstar alter ego (who was known to make a regular appearance). Instead, I opt for a light tapping of the steering wheel and occasional tut at the careless motoring decisions of others.

8.58 a.m.: I check my wing mirror and drift across into the slow lane. 8.59 a.m.: I fill my lungs with as much air conditioning as I have available. 9 a.m.: time to hit the big green button next to our social worker's name. She picks up almost immediately, giving me no time to prepare my greeting, resulting in me skipping one altogether and bombarding her with last night's sleepless thoughts on the little boy with the striped sock who we hadn't stopped thinking about and while we were following all professional advice in not getting attached at this stage, I'm really worried his socks aren't on tight enough. She laughs, asks me to slow down, and in among the professional nitty gritty necessities of a phone call such as this comes recognition from her that we've felt an intense connection with a child. So, I have to ask of her that she do everything within her professional power to help us bring him home.

Before I go on, I feel a level of responsibility to admit that the process beyond the point of feeling a connection with a child doesn't always run smooth. It's been said the course of true love never did. It simply may not run at all; you could feel such an overwhelming sense of belonging and wanting for a child you've learnt about, but that doesn't necessarily mean the child's social worker is going to feel the same way about you. Prospective adopters feeling they've found their match will find that only takes them 50 per cent of the way there.

Remember this is about finding *the right family for the child* regardless of the connection you may have felt. This isn't about *you*, as hard as that may be to accept. If you're unsuccessful, then at that stage you must try to take solace in knowing the child has been matched with the people or person believed to be right for them and that child has found permanence.

Then eat lots of ice-cream and cry because you're not a robot.

You could make it down to the wire, social workers may have filtered you down to the final two prospective choices (this is called competitive matching – you read that right) for the child, but one of you will be left empty. Then there's the matching panel hurdle. Yes, there is yet *another* panel of professionals to convince that you are deserving to parent the child or children – as there should be. I don't dispute the relentless demands of the process, but you can simultaneously have both the utmost respect and feel exhaustion for a process that does not exclusively operate between the hours of 9–5 and will encroach into every waking (and sleepless) second of your existence until you reach the finish line.

There's also the subject of time. More specifically the timeframes between the moment you are linked with a child until you are matched, between matching and introductions. This could be weeks if an Early Permanence placement; however, I have known of circumstances whereby a year has elapsed and the cruel reality of life can sometimes mean landscapes change. Be it financial, critical illness, bereavement, a sudden relationship breakdown. Anything could happen, that's the uncertainty which could tragically impact the outcome.

I suppose I want to let it be known that our course to true love was fraught, uneven, rough and hirsute (thank you, Google). My very wise publisher educated me on what the word 'author' means: 'to give authorisation'; and while I've granted that in offering such intimate moments of my life in a bid to comfort others, in truth, I am the only person with the authority to make that decision. I ask for your camaraderie, dear readers, as I attempt to draw my story to a close while respectfully not stepping past lines that don't belong to me.

Guilty, Your Honour

We'd been asked to write a supporting document on why we should be considered the right match for the magical little boy with the captivating eyes. I didn't know I could even write until we'd been asked to do this. It's remarkable what you can achieve when you really want something or *someone*. When it comes to the crunch and you're asked to write for a chance of becoming a mother, it's *that* text that could become your greatest work. We wrote with the only crafts-manship either of us really had to offer: honesty. And if I were to advise anyone else in our situation, I would say do the same. Write from your heart to theirs. Write as their greatest advocate, parent and best friend because when you're writing to love a brave stranger, friendship will prove a safe place to start.

We'd filled the time with regularly annoying our social worker for updates she didn't have (I'd be inter-ested to know exactly how far off a restraining order we were) while prepping for the tropical painkiller and body pump classes. My husband and I would lie to each other nightly about the number of times we'd looked at his photograph throughout the day, giving each other a considerably lower number. We were aware that we needed to protect ourselves from decisions being made by faraway people in faraway offices that remained very much out of our control. There's a comment often made when going through the adoption process that could give the old '*just relax*' during infertility a run for its money: '*Enjoy all this free time you have because your life could change in an instant.*' If I may, I'd just like to take this moment of your time to let it be known that, for the majority of those who've completed months' worth of assessments, showing doctors we can touch our knees and reaching out to exes we'd really rather not, we are here because we *want* our lives to change in an instant and all this '*free time*' has proved very difficult to '*enjoy*'.

I've managed to accessorise myself with a rather large chalazion on my right eyelid just before we go away. I've never been much of a trendsetter but as such cysts are known to hang around for months, I embrace the look with a warm compress hidden behind a variety of different sunglasses. We arrive at the ticket office for the Heathrow Express, cotton pads flying out of my handbag as I fumble around in search of my purse. I'm met with a rather bemused member of staff wondering how far up my own arse I must be for wearing shades inside when outside isn't far off a hurricane, and I clearly can't see a bloody thing. As she slides two return tickets across the counter, I feel the vibration of my phone from the abyss of my handbag and continue the diva attitude she believes me to have by offering a swift 'thank you' in order to reach my phone in time.

I read our social worker's name and signal my husband to put down the snacks he doesn't need for the fifteen-minute journey ahead of him and to come over to the phone I'm about to answer.

'*Hello.*'

'*Hello.*'

'*How are you?*' (It's meant well but jeez, in this instance, politeness really isn't necessary. I'd rather she just cut to the chase.)

'*Good, thank you, and you?*' (Total hypocrite.)

'*Good news, his social worker would like to come and visit you as soon as possible. When are you back?*'

Don't wish your life or holiday away. Every day is a gift. Which of course it is, but never have I been sitting in a departure lounge ahead of a thirteen-hour flight willing it to be the return journey. I couldn't help but shamefully stare down at my newly painted toes feeling such guilt for flying further away from the little boy whom we did not yet have the privilege of responsibility to feel guilty about, but I wanted him to be more than anything in the world. This could be my first taste of the 'mum guilt' I'd heard so much about and was always envious of those who had it. I *wanted* mum guilt in abundance. I wanted him to know we would be back, how we wouldn't be gone for long and although he didn't have my number or the cognitive ability to make a phone call, he *could* call me if he needed anything. As the plane took to the sky and we broke through the well-hidden sunshine up into the clouds I made a promise to him. Wherever he was, whoever he was with, we would do our damnedest to prove to his social worker that we would fight for him, on the day they would come to visit and every day we had left. For the rest of our lives.

We had ten long days ahead to try to absorb some of the vibrancy surrounding us. The first five we spent in Havana rehydrating only with white rum and sugar, a soulful, raw place, full of narrow streets and a rainbow of colourful buildings. A city where dancing in the street is the norm, any time of the day, and being serenaded by guitars can be a spontaneous act not wheeled out solely for romantic occasions. I watched my husband smoke cigars the size of a rolling pin; we had a salsa lesson resulting in less of the 'quick, quick' and a predominant focus on the 'slow'. We laughed at his two left feet and my bulging eye. I wasn't a fan of the food, he's never not. The only Cuban food group we could agree on were the frozen Daiquiris.

We took photos of 1950s American cars in nearly every colour, pretended not to be lost and walked through someone's house and hanging laundry to get to a *paladar* (small family-owned restaurants that were illegal up until the 1990s). We'd talk about the little boy with an element of self-preservation *before* a frozen Daiquiri but by the third, we were discussing how to break the news to the grandparents. The following five days were spent in an all-inclusive in Mexico.

As soon as we arrive, I head straight for a sun

lounger with a plateful of pastries, connect to some long-awaited Wi-Fi and smear on the highest factor sun cream my pasty little hands can get hold of. My husband flip-flops ahead with his Jenga tower of chosen treats. Just as I get myself into the optimum sunbathing, pastry-eating position, the sound of my phone interrupts the cascading of crisp flakes. I scroll through my notifications, shifting through a good amount of junk emails. One was really very kind; I'd won 50,000 gold bars, they just needed my bank details, passport information and address. A text from my dad asking if we'd got there OK and a larger file sent by our social worker.

We'd only seen that one photograph of him so far. Just one, but it was the only one we needed to know how much we wanted to be in his life. She's sent us another five or six and my stomach double flips with excitement. I try to string an audible sentence together to my husband but it's really not easy with a mouth full of croissant and a stomach full of butterflies. I sort of squeal and hold up the phone, he jumps across to my lounger. We look at his photographs in *awe*. Taking a breath, not breathing and we look once more, just in case we've missed any tiny little bit about him, and again because we can't not.

The rest of the afternoon is spent huddling together on that one lounger talking about him. Practising what we would say to his social worker when she came round and pointlessly reminding ourselves not to get too attached at this stage. A reminder that's about as useful as a chocolate fireguard. We were attached, end of.

Guilty, your honour.

Our fireguards melted weeks ago and if we've unwrapped our hearts before we should have done, then so be it. He's more than worth it and we tried to be OK with the prospect of us never amounting to more than two strangers on a sun lounger thinking about him. Because he deserved to be thought of from every sun lounger, in every corner of the world.

Later that afternoon we find ourselves lost in a foam party. A precautionary act. *Just in case* this was to be our last, *child-free* holiday.

A Lion and a Mouse
Sit Down to Tea

Most of you can relate to the feeling of utter horror when a friend calls on the hop to say they're only five minutes away and thought it would be 'nice' to pop in. The reality is there's nothing 'nice' about creeping up on someone unannounced, ever. Come on, we all know that when we've been *invited*, what we're actually stepping into is a false reality with clear draining boards and clothes in cupboards. Well, it's this very same feeling of anxiety when a social worker invites themselves over to assess a potential match. I felt it even with ample notice and assurances from others that it won't come down to how clean my windows are. I knew perfectly bleached toilets and empty floordrobes wouldn't be the clincher but in the days leading up to her arrival, I just couldn't help myself. You ought to know that a social worker will not base the potential for you to parent on which cleaning products you use, no matter how ethical or eco-friendly. However, in times of great anxiety we revert to our preferred coping mechanisms. Bleaching the crap out of toilets (literally) was mine.

I'd scrubbed, decluttered, organised and bleached before strategically de-organising (so as not to look neurotic) every room in the house. Walls were considering themselves lucky to have held onto even one coat of their paint by the time I'd finished. Every room, that was, apart from one.

His.

At least, the one we *hoped* to be his.

I couldn't move a thing.

I open the door one last time before she's due to arrive. The door to a room we had prepared for a child we didn't really know but who'd taken our every waking thought of late. I'm met with smiling lions, tall giraffes and the odd random ostrich running along the wallpaper; I hoped he might like safari animals. I stand in a swirl of freshly painted mushroom greys, neutral earthy browns and soft yellows. I savour the smell of wood from the pre-loved nursery furniture courtesy of Grooveybabz85! Her 'excellent condition' description was true to its word. Above my head hangs a paper hot-air balloon light shade, with a tiny passenger teddy snuggled into its basket underneath the bulb.

I won't allow myself more than just a few steps inside to flick a polishing cloth halfway round the rim of an empty cot and check in on teddy, making sure he's tucked safely into his basket. I do allow myself a private moment before strangers form their opinion. Closing my eyes, taking a deep breath in, praying to a God I wasn't sure I believed in.

When I'm done bartering with the ceiling, I close the door behind me. I have to wait until my legs grant me the strength to make this final trip away from a room I've filled with dreams. Dreams maybe I shouldn't have, because there's every chance that, after this visit, I would have to let them decay.

Our family finder advised we have a cake baking in the oven for when they arrived. Something to do with the psychology behind a home being more inviting with the sweet smell of sugar baking away. A theory I won't dispute, only the smoke alarm goes off quite a bit in our house. Particularly when my husband's let loose on the griddle pan. Not sure if that's the ambience she's after. A cake felt too ambitious given the nerves, although maybe it's all just a ploy to calm them, giving me an activity to focus on.

There was truth for me personally in what she had suggested. Advice that triggered those skittish, after school, key-twisting-in-the-lock moments wondering what welcome I was to receive. If I could smell warm sugar, mixed with spices and baked raisins, I knew she was having a 'good day'. One where she *could* love me and had the capacity to ask about school. Playfully teasing me about boys I didn't fancy and threatening girls who might be causing me grief. She'd thrust a sugar-coated lump of rock cake or fruit scone under my nose demanding I tried it *immediately* before wanting a review on just *how good* they were on a scale of one to ten. Did they need more or less sugar? Were there enough raisins? Had she overcooked them slightly? The answers, my friends, were always: Ten. Just the right amount. Yes and No.

She was the first person to teach me how to bake. Scones, I can remember her teaching me how to bake scones. I recall watching her gold wedding band become disguised by flour and lumps of sugary butter. Her teaching me how to roll out the dough, how to sprinkle snowflakes of flour on the surface and rolling pin first to avoid the dough sticking. She taught me how you don't even need to have a cutter and would always use the rim of a glass. I have familiar memories of her baking bowl. A large, light brown, ceramic bowl with white interior. A cardigan knitted print embossed along the outside. I recall watching her mixing ingredients in that bowl with absolute determination. Me perched beside her, like a seagull waiting for the go-ahead to lick the wooden spoon.

There were some good days with that cardigan bowl.

As I look for a glass to cut the best scones known to man or social worker, I can't help but smile.

Five of us are sitting round our kitchen table that afternoon (a table that really ought to write its own book). Me, my husband, our social worker and two representatives for the magical little boy. Three of them seem to enjoy eating warm scones topped with jam and cream. Two of us pretend to have an interest in where the cream was sourced and how many calories we reckoned were in a cream tea. They start with professional small talk, a strategic approach. An attempt at trying to get us to relax, to give them the most authentic version of ourselves. Allowing them to decipher whether the child we'd been talking and thinking about every waking minute, for what's felt like eternity, was to become our son. Eventually they push the crumbs, pleasantries and cream-covered knives to the side to get down to the *real* reason we're all sitting here today. They ask questions we've never been asked before and some we've already answered in our written statement. At times they're asking the same questions worded differently. We respond and give our answers again. These remain the same even in response to their rotating sentences. This dance repeats itself for quite a while. I can feel the eyes of one social worker closely watching us as we respond. This leads me to keep awkwardly turning my head to smile at her. They ask if we have any questions. We have so many, but the one of most importance, the only one that *really matters* to us both, is:

'*How is he?*'

They smile and answer our most precious question. My husband and I savour every word, squeezing one another's hand under the privacy of our trusty table, him stroking mine and me his as they continue to talk while sharing information and photographs we hadn't yet seen. I notice there is a video. It suddenly occurs to me that we have never seen him move. We have no idea if he still stumbles when he tries to walk, or what his little fingers look like when he reaches out, does he throw his head back when he laughs or frown when he's cross?

It begins.

He moves.

I hear a kind voice filled with encouragement coming, I assume, from his foster carer.

Foster carers, people who open up their hearts and homes to love and protect some of this country's most vulnerable children, round the clock, twenty-four hours a day. The government is effectively accountable for these children and in return only a small minority of foster carers (thought to be one in ten) is in receipt of the equivalent of the national living wage for a forty-hour week. A survey carried out by the Fostering Network in 2017 revealed that, based on this forty-hour week, a quarter of foster carers received the equivalent of less than £1.70 an hour.[16] One in eight fostering households quit in 2022 due to the cost-of-living crisis according to Ofsted.[17]

I want to respond with something mildly intellectual but all I have to offer is: what the (enter expletive here) goes on during these parliamentary children's social care meetings?

When will the childcare system become a government priority?

When will *society* show the system matters enough for government to make it a priority?

(All political frustrations expressed here are my own.)

You're very welcome to discuss the points raised over dinner.

And yes, that was my (peaceful) political call to arms. Now, back to the kitchen table.

*

We've never been so desperate to see something but unable to look. We sit shamefully hanging our heads at not being able to look at him. Tears rolling from our cheeks landing onto little bits of crumbs, desperately trying not to show the cats how we don't want to play today. We don't want to be teased with sounds of a little voice we may never get to hear, watch little hands we might never get to hold.

I want to look but am terrified at the thought of never being able to forget seeing him. Like a mouse, I remain frozen, avoiding the bright lights of the iPad, the noise of a voice I want to listen to forever, and try to make myself as small as possible.

My husband won't be the mouse, not today.

He's far braver than me in telling them the truth as he chokes back words and holds back tears. Explaining how he simply *can't watch*. Just in case.

A lion and a mouse sit down to tea. The lion's heart is breaking but he won't let them see.

I can feel the analytical watch of their eyes as I hear the iPad slide back across the table and the quick zip of a bag as it's packed away. There's a few moments of silence from all round the table before a request to have a look around the rest of the house. I spring up like one of those cheap frogs you get out of a Christmas cracker, ready to showcase my cleaning efforts. I talk far too much and give an unnecessarily extended version of the tour, inclusive of the linen cupboard. By the time we make it to our bedroom she politely explains how she doesn't need to come all the way in. This means I won't get to show her my husband's folded underpants. She's probably OK with that, but when you know something will never look that good again, you *need* someone to witness it.

Then comes the room I want her to see the most. The one I'm going to make sure she steps *all* the way inside. This is the only corner of the house that really matters, and I don't care if *she* feels she doesn't need to see all of it, *I* need her to. I open the door and usher her in first. That way I can act as a barricade to her making her way back out. It's not a hostage situation or anything, she can leave at any point, if she asks.

'*This is* his *room.*'

That's what came out. It just fell out of my mouth, and once it had, I couldn't take it back. I decided this wasn't the time to worry if I'd made a fool of myself. If this were to be another foolish moment of hope to add to my *Quest to Motherhood* album, then so be it. I had no reputation to lose but the privilege of a little life to gain, so I just carried on. Explaining how we'd paid attention to what characters he liked and thought about what he might need. I showed her the teddies and the giant giraffe, the books and the paper hot-air balloon. We stayed in this room the longest.

She never asked to leave.

Eventually they did leave. Saying nothing, giving nothing away. Not even so much as a knowing smile or disappointed sigh. They just professionally depart, leaving us in a state of cluelessness waving them off the driveway. They leave us and crack on with the really important, life-altering decisions they have to make every day.

I make my way back upstairs to overanalyse every single thing I said and fold up my pants. I don't like the idea of his drawer being neater than mine.

Orcas

Life carries on after a visit like that. Washing machines still spin, bills need to be paid and team-building boot camps must be attended and I'm the lucky recruit summoned to enrol on one of these over the next few days. Lured in with the promise of a two-night stay in a wooden shepherd's hut and a branded company onesie, I have to bunk up with a work colleague I've never met and pretend to be bowled over (no pun intended) by the complimentary cereal selection pack. I'm unable to sleep a wink for sheer excitement at what the organisation could *possibly* have planned for Q3 and Q4.

I was to be apart from my husband for the next forty-eight hours knowing we were waiting for the most important phone call of our lives over that period. I'd also be asked to stand in front of other onesie-wearing colleagues expected to perform an improvised rap, praising the company vision round a campfire.

Readers, that's not even the shocking part.

That *winning* rap earned me a personalised

snapback company cap and a photo opportunity with the CEO.

I don't sleep much; my roomie's a snorer (I only speak in rap now). The first night is spent scrolling through social media, stalking old school friends, monotonously swiping past smiling photos of them with their children. Reading every comment under the photo of a colleague who's off on maternity leave, again. For a change of theme, I open my camera roll and zoom in on our wedding photos trying to work out exactly how much this quest to parenthood has aged us and if I need to start cheap Botox. I'm only in the market for cheap. (You definitely shouldn't ever do that; it's a poor attempt at humour. Go medically qualified and if they're cheap it's a bonus.)

I restlessly lie there. Staring up at the pine ceiling. Hours of digital blue light hasn't helped my sleep campaign. When I do close my eyes, I see visions of him, tucked up in his bed, snuggly and warm. Wondering what the print on his blanket looks like. Is he even in a blanket or one of those sleeping bag things? Do his curls stick to his sweaty head at night? Then I get up the next morning, treat myself to another helping of Coco Pops and pretend I'm not waiting for someone to tell me today, maybe even tomorrow, if I'm about to become a mother to a little boy who's growing not in my womb but in *my heart*.

The morning consists of team-building exercises, a compliment circle and company quiz. By lunchtime I'm all complimented out and opt to have my cheese and pickle sandwich alone back at the hut. I make my way past the less-than-healthy-looking lake, brushing my sandwich-free hand through the tall reeds, debating if it's too early to call my husband, aware that he usually breaks later. I feel the vibration of my phone in the pocket of my denim shorts. I fumble around trying to grab it, which shouldn't be this difficult given how small the pocket is. This is what happens when I'm anxious, my brain to limb connection just takes the day off. Our social worker's name flashes across the screen. I stare at it for a second then look up to gauge exactly how far away I am from some hut privacy. I'm really not sure if I'll be able to contain my emotions from either outcome she's about to give me so make a run towards the glass door. I answer the phone but I don't speak immediately, not until I've reached the security of the shepherd's hut.

'*Hi.*'

I fling open the door to the hut.

'*Sorry, I was running.*'

—

I'm panting.

She's laughing.

'*I won't drag this out for you.*'

I close my eyes and I fill my lungs with the last breath of unknowing air.

'*They think you're a good match.*'

The weight of my body evaporates, legs crumbling to the floor below me, hands barely able to keep hold of the phone.

I whimper, the same way I'd witnessed my husband do all those months ago. I whimper thank-yous and mutterings of disbelief down the phone to the woman who had played her part in this fight. Who believed in a couple who only ever wanted to love. Who'd guided, advised and advocated for us with such invested belief when we told her this child was the one.

I whimper and she lets me.

When we're done

I lie alone.

—

Allowing my body to finally rest, lying motionless on the wooden floor to which I had fallen knowing: *I. Had. Survived.* Breathing intermittently through my nostrils, sporadically inhaling gasps of air. The stillness of my eyeball reflecting on the glass door I'd burst through just moments before. Mammals do not cry, the only exception being us, human beings. They hurt, they have to fight to survive, and perhaps the greatest thing uniting us all is the primal urge to love and be loved. If we ignore our human ego, we could come to realise *all* creatures look to love, and are we not all just creatures?

—

I blearily look beyond the open door, beyond the lake and tall reeds, up to the clouds resting in the sky and release my long-suffocated call from the primal depth of my soul.

The call of a mother to her son.
Like an orca to her calf.
Needing the ocean to know she has found him.
Orcas live in complex family pods and swim beside their children all their lives.

—

My life's greatest honour will be to swim beside you for the rest of mine.

I called this book *What Makes a Mum?* as an invitation to sit with me and listen to one woman's story.
I believe motherhood is not a symbol of status.
Or a statement of ownership.
But an evolving feeling of the greatest love.
A privilege and an honour.
Oh, and the pound given to me from the helpful woodlouse? That was for my son to take a kiddie ride outside a supermarket.

This has been my journey of maternal evolution.
So far . . .

'You're here', said Motherhood.
'Sorry I'm so late, I wasn't sure I'd ever make it'.
Not a Fictional Mum.

Over the next decade the number of children in care
is predicted to reach 100,000.

Acknowledgements

Kicking this off thanking my best friend and simply wonderful human, my husband, who endured living with me and my laptop for nearing two years. I absolutely adore you. My son, you're just brilliance, in every sense. My beautiful Dad, the Little Armadillo, my Perfect Stranger and the woman who looked beyond her fears and fostered a girl who needed you. Thank you.

To my agent Hannah Ferguson of Hardman & Swainson for your consistent belief in my story, supporting me as a mother and writer. You really are very good at your job and deserve a promotion with immediate effect. My publishers at Unbound for taking the words I never imagined writing and giving them life in print, making me an *actual* author.

To my developmental editor Rachael Kerr for your care and understanding, enduring my crying on zoom (multiple times). Copy-editor Tamsin Shelton and proofreader Sarah Bance, you had your work cut out there (huge amount of grammatical respect). Finally, my editor Marissa Constantinou for your continued patience throughout my moments of self-doubt and submission deadlines. You also deserve a promotion.

Each of my sensitivity readers who kindly looked upon my words with their hearts, wisdom and experience. I'm very grateful. My testimonials, Lisa Faulkner, Giovanna Fletcher, Rochelle Humes and Anna Mather. Women only too willing to lift up an unknown woman's voice. The online sisterhoods a pretty powerful one.

To Emma Simpson CEO of CCS Adoption for her professional support and guidance on relevant text.

Every supporter of the Self-Employed Adopter's Campaign and those who've stood beside Not a Fictional Mum in parliament. An endless thank you to the entire team from our Voluntary Adoption Agency.

Huge thank you to my lovely Book Patrons; The Modern Family Show, Cover My Bubble, CCS adoption and The Fertility Show. Shout out to my ex-local-authority for pledging their support and to every single supporter of this book. Those who gave their name for print and those who remain anonymous.

You've all been instrumental in bringing this book to publication: *thank you all,* so very, much.

Book Recommendations

Lisa Faulkner, *Meant to Be: My Journey to Motherhood*

Rosalind Powell, *How I Met My Son: A Journey through Adoption*

Jessica Hepburn, *The Pursuit of Motherhood* (and basically anything else she has written and recorded)

Sally Donovan, *No Matter What: An Adoptive Family's Story of Hope, Love and Healing*

Louise Allen, *How to Adopt a Child: Your Step-by-step Guide to Adopting and Parenting*

Notes

1 'Infertility', NHS Wales, 111.wales.nhs.uk/encyclopaedia/i/article/infertility/
2 'IVF', NHS, www.nhs.uk/conditions/ivf/
3 'Egg freezing patients "misled" by clinics' by Anna Collinson, Maryam Ahmed and Bella McShane, BBC News, www.bbc.co.uk/news/uk-68505321
4 'Make self-employed people eligible for statutory adoption pay', Petitions, UK Government and Parliament, petition.parliament.uk/petitions/601323
5 'Support for New Adoptive Parents', Volume 711: debated on Monday 21 March 2022, Hansard, UK Parliament, hansard.parliament.uk/commons/2022-03-21/debates/42C1D133-9CEF-482D-994F-5F971FFB8BC4/SupportForNewAdoptiveParents
6 'My parents at war: Jacqueline Wilson opens up about unhappy early life' by Donna Ferguson, *Guardian*, www.theguardian.com/books/2016/sep/24/jacqueline-wilson-unhappy-childhood-tracy-beaker
7 'Miscarriage', NHS, www.nhs.uk/conditions/miscarriage/
8 'Ofsted to start registering supported accommodation providers from April' by Ofsted, www.gov.uk/government/news/ofsted-to-start-registering-supported-accommodation-providers-from-april
9 'Why the wait ... in 2023', Home for Good, homeforgood.org.uk/why-the-wait

10 'Placement stability and permanence', Fostering and Adoption Research in Practice, fosteringandadoption.rip.org.uk

11 'Time to say sorry', Adoption UK, www.adoptionuk.org/blog/time-to-say-sorry

12 'How many adoptions break down', Adoption UK, www.adoptionuk.org/faqs/how-many-adoptions-break-down

13 'In Focus: Independent review of children's social care' by Emily Haves, House of Lords Library, UK Parliament, lordslibrary.parliament.uk/independent-review-of-childrens-social-care/

14 'DfE provides 20% of funding urged by care review in response' by Mithran Samuel, Community Care, www.communitycare.co.uk/2023/02/02/dfe-provides-20-of-funding-urged-by-care-review-in-response/

15 'Council faces projected £68M overspend', City of Bradford Metropolitan District Council, www.bradford.gov.uk/browse-all-news/press-releases/council-faces-projected-68m-overspend/

16 'Foster carer pay', The Fostering Network, www.thefostering network.org.uk/get-involved/our-campaigns/foster-carer-pay-o

17 'One in eight fostering households quit last year, finds Ofsted' by Anastasia Koutsounia, Community Care, www.community care.co.uk/2022/11/25/one-in-eight-fostering-households-quit-2022-ofsted/

Unbound is the world's first crowdfunding publisher, established in 2011.

We believe that wonderful things can happen when you clear a path for people who share a passion. That's why we've built a platform that brings together readers and authors to crowdfund books they believe in – and give fresh ideas that don't fit the traditional mould the chance they deserve.

This book is in your hands because readers made it possible. Everyone who pledged their support is listed below. Join them by visiting unbound.com and supporting a book today.

Laura Abernethy
Martha Adam-Bushell
Joanna Agate
Safeera Ahmed
Emily Allen
Emma Allen
Naomi Anderson
Jennifer Anderton
Sarah Andrew
Hayley Andrews
Lois Andrews
Dough Animal
Becky Aqua

Armadillo
Jennifer Armstrong
Amy Ashby
Karyn & Lilly Badger
Hannah Bailey
Karen Bailey
Nicky Baker
Rachel Balfour-Mears
Audrey Balmain
Katie Bannister
Ella Barnett
Joana Barros
Louise Baughan

Caitlin Bawn
Mommy Bear
Ross Beasley
Michelle Bendall
Jen Bennett
Kathryn Bennett
James & Kate Birchett
Polly Boardman
H Bonner-Smith
Emma Bothma
Sharon Boundy
Mr & Mrs Bowers
Rachael and Paul
	Brackenridge
Jenny Bradshaw
Mary Brennan
Jennifer Briant
Sarah Briant
Lynne Brown
Sara Joy Brown
Tia Brown
Brian Browne
Rachel Browne
Katy Brunton
Laurie Buckham
Laura Buckingham
@bumpyroadmum
Abi Burt
Jem Burton
Holly Butler
Moona Butt

Rosemarie Buttery
Kevin Button
Caroline Louise Byrne
Jenni Cain
Kirstie Caine
Alice Caithness
Debi Cale
Kate Calloway
Sara Calver
Lindy Cameron-
	Saunders
Hannah Campbell
Rebecca Campbell
Sally Camps
Foster Carer
Carly, Martin, Zephyr,
	Sol
Jessica Carter
Katy Carter
Stephanie Casaubon @
	adoptionislove_book
Sarah Caswell
Kirsten Cavey
Lindsay Chandler
Vandita Chandrani
Amelie Chaplin
Jess & Jo Chappell
Paula Chidgey
Vicki Child
Julie Chilton
Chloe

Sandy Christiansen
Kitty Clark
Naomi Clark
Kelly Clements
Sarah Clutton
Lisa Colledge
Rachel Colley
Charlotte Conway
Zoe Cooke
Danielle Cooper
Nick Cooper
Karly Cooper-Baker
Sorcha Cotter
Laura Coupland
Catherine Cowell
CraftyChopsCornwall
   (Claire)
Ros Croker-Ahmed
Suzanne Crompton
Amy & Kirsty
   Crossland-Browne
Sophie Crowther
Michelle Cruden Brown
Sinéad Cummings
Liz Cunningham-
   Purchall
Danielle Curran
Alice Daniel
Rishi Dastidar
Jenny Davies
Nathalie Davies

Sara Dawson
Rachel de Minckwitz
Nicola Dervey
Preeti Dhillon
Alexandra Dickinson
Sarah Dimond
Shannon Dodd
Sophia Donata Walton
Charlotte Doran
Zoë Down
Charlotte Dubois
Rachel Dungate
Helen Dunn
Camille Dupont
Clare Eason
Lucy Edis
Hayley Ellingham
Victoria Rose Ellis
Joanne Else
Emma
Antonia Emmins
Ems
Erica Evans
Gemma Evans
Lisa Evans
Jennifer Farrell
Lisa Faulkner
Hannah Ferguson
Nicola FitzGerald
Katherine Flannery
Ashley Fleming

Sophie Flynn
For Ruby Tuesday
Michelle Fox
Alexa Franklin-Slattery
Lizzy Fraser
Nic Freem
Joeleen Fyfe
Jane Gardner
Amaryllis Garland
Kirsty Gelder Smith
Caz Gentleman
Celyse George-Gordon
Felicity Gibbs
Fay Gkontosidou
Turd Glitterer
Lyndsey Glynn
Keeley Gordon
Claire Gough
Emma Grange
Jennifer Greatorex
Danielle Green
Sarah Greenan
Jade Greene
Sally Greenwood
Rebecca Grimshaw
Joanne Grubb
Beth Gubbins
Julie Guihen
Katie Gwynn
Michelle Hall
Jo Handoll

Cara Hannan
Sam Harding
Emily Hardy
Emma Hardy
Shelley Harlock
Vicky Harman
Traceyann Harper
Rosy Harrington
Laura Harrison
Lyndel Harrison
Lauren Hart
Louise Harvey
Joslyn Haydon
Alison Haynes
Claire Henderson
Sarah Hensby
Jessica Hepburn
Amanda Hickling
Vicky Higgs
Rachel Hobbs
Hollie
Kat Holmes
Sarah Hopkins
Poppy Horwill
@House_Proud_Dads
Jo How
Molly Howell
Pauline Hoyle
Sophie Huey
Brenda Hughes
Kathryn Hughes

Megan Hughes
Lisa Huish
Brona Hulme
Emma Hunt
Ellie Hutchinson
Rachel Hyde
Abi Iles
Emma Inman
Kaleigh Isaac
Katie Jackson
Trixie Jardine
Kirsty Jay
Carys Jeffery
Leyanne Jenkins
Sophie Jenkins
Faye Jeray
Joadie
Gwawr Job-Davies
Leigh Johnson
Lisa Johnston
Alex Jones
Laura Jones
Mrs Katherine Jones
Rachel Jones
Rebecca Jones
Katie
Elizabeth Keating
Rhiannon Kelland
Julie-Ann Kelly
Siobhan Kelly
Lauren Kendall

Sophie Kendall
Laura Keohane
Elizabeth King
Lydia King
Samantha King
Julia Kirkham
Jordanna
    Kissoon-Carr
Janice Knox
Louise Kuvelker
Lottie Lagerman
Lindsey Lancaster
Fay Lant
Lucy Leake
Bethan Lee
Clare Lee
Rosemary Leigh
Lyndsay Lennie
Fiona Lensvelt
Ann Leonard
Karen Levens
Suzy Levy
Amy Lewis
Lindsey Lewis
Elizabeth Lightowler
Dawn Limitsios
Hannah Lincoln
Darran Lincolnshaw
Jen Lister
Holly Lucas
Vivien Luckhurst

Hannah M-R
Sarrah Macey
Louise Mackie
Gemma MacMillan
Nicola Maison
Emma Makepeace
Christine Malloch
Natasha Mardle
Anna Marsh
Becky Martin-Vass
Anna Mathur
Bex May
Caroline Mayes
Mary Catherine
   Mc Ardle
Elaine McCreath
Patrica Mcdonagh
Clare McDonald
Louise McEwen
Victoria McGlen
Maeve McGlinchey
Ashley McGowan
Louise McGrath
Leanne McGuire
Clare McHatton
Louise Mclady
Brian Mcleish
Kirstin McRae-Smith
Colleen McSorley
Marie Meadows
Michelle

Heidi Micic
Emily Milne
Louise Minty
Katie Mitchell
John Mitchinson
Lisa Moe
Claire Moffitt
Jenni Moody
Laura Moore
Sarah Moore
Jessica Morley
Mary Morris
Karen Moses
Zara Mufti
Jillian Mullen
Jennifer Murray
La Música
Eve MW
Carlo Navato
Rebecca Nazareth
Stephanie Neal
Fiona Neeson
Kirsty Neil
Nikki Newlister
Amy Newton
Laurence Nicolay
Vanessa Noble
Victoria Noble
Rachel O'Connor
Ana O'Reilly
Candy Oberbeck

Laura Offer
Gillian OHare
Rachael Oku
Natalie Olivey
Lisa Orrell
Bernie Osborne
Jennifer Osborne
Amy Owen
Julie Owen
Valerie Paisey
Anna Palmer
Serena Parker-Sharp
Aimee Parnham
Rebecca Pasha
Lisa Pay
Sandra Pell
Fiona Penny
Hugo Perks
Alice Perry
Hannah Perry
Elizabeth Petrichor
Jen Pettigrew
Eleanor Phillips
Rachel Phillips
Eleri Phillips Adams
Rebekah Pierre
Fleur Pijpers
Pip
Kirsty Pipkin
Gemma Pitman
Natasha Plummer

Plymouth City Council
    Care Leavers Team
Louise Pocock
Steven Potter
Catriona Powell
Nikki Powell
Sophie Power
April Prasad
Julie Pullen
Jennifer Purdon
Carina Raimbach
James Rands
Katie Raper
Sarah Rathburn
Sherrill Redfern
Arwel Rees-Taylor
Suzi Robertson
Eleanor Robinson
Keely Robinson
Rayanne Robinson
LJ Robson
Jenny Rolfe
Laura Rollo-Smith
Jennifer Rolph
Dilly Rose
Pauline Rosie
Olivia Rowe
Annette Rule
Kerry Rushton-
    Hinchliffe
Gaby S

Linda Sampson
Nicole Sandler
Hannah Sansom
Vera Santos
Emily Saunders
Jami Saunders
Hannah Sawyer
Victoria Saxby-Edwards
Alex Sayer
Laura Sellars
Jeff Seneviratne
Selina Shaw
Jennifer Shirley
Tash Shirley
Kim Shore
Kirsty Short
Lisa Shotton
Teresa Silvas
Ana Silveira
Alison Simms
Kelly Simpson
Sian Simpson
Skye
Rachel Slaughter
Milly Smythe
Gillian Somerville
Emma Speer
Clare Spence
Catriona Spiers Bennett
Emma Spillane
Sinead Spratt

Jen Stafford
Alison Steel
Mackenna Stevenson
S E Stewart
Rebecca Stockdale
Becky Stockting-Watts
Helen Stokes
Vicky Stoll
Perfect Stranger
Hannah Stroud
Iain Stuart
Laura Summers
Dawn Swinburne
Gail Sykes
Kayleigh Tang
Aimee Targett
Chloë Tarr
Claire Taylor
Karen Taylor
Lydia Taylor
Natasha Taylor
Wendy Taylor
Lottie Teideman
The Kirby's Journey
Estelle Thomas
Amber Thompson
Krissy Thompson
Lucy Thorn
Lowri Thornley
Emma Thornton
Katy Thoroughgood

Beth Threlfall-Rogers
Ruth Till
Hannah Tincombe
Laura Tinsley
Felicity Tomkins
Marianne Tomsa
L. Toner
Lynsey Travers
Carol Tully
Fiona Tweedie
Stefano Vermonti
Rachael Vidal
Elouise Waind
Shula Waining
Nicola Wake
Aileen Walker
Sarah Walker
Amelia Walsh
Emily Ward
Sara Warry-Powell
Hannah Warwick
Emma Watkin
Rhiannon Watson
Alison Watts

Wayne, Ian and
    Albert
Rebecca Weaver
Robyn Weston
Daisy Whitbread
Katie White
Kristina Whyman
Louise Wicks
Rebecca Wilkins
Emma Williams
Gaynor Williamson
Hannah Williamson
Mrs Winkleberry
Michael Wofff
Wogie and Liza
Hannah Woods
Sarah Woolford
Louise Wright
Katie Wylie
Sophie Yale
Jacky Yardley
Laura Young
Suzzie Z.
Elizabeth Zappia